Greyhounds

Greyhound Dogs Complete Owner's Guide

Greyhound Basics, Choosing and Owning, Breeding, Care, Feeding, Grooming, Showing and Training All Included!

By: Lolly Brown

Copyrights and Trademarks

All rights reserved. No part of this book may be reproduced or transformed in any form or by any means, graphic, electronic, or mechanical, including photocopying, recording, taping, or by any information storage retrieval system, without the written permission of the author.

This publication is Copyright ©2022 NRB Publishing, an imprint of Pack & Post Plus, LLC. Nevada. All products, graphics, publications, software and services mentioned and recommended in this publication are protected by trademarks. In such instance, all trademarks & copyright belong to the respective owners. For information consult www.NRBpublishing.com

Disclaimer and Legal Notice

This product is not legal, medical, or accounting advice and should not be interpreted in that manner. You need to do your own due-diligence to determine if the content of this product is right for you. While every attempt has been made to verify the information shared in this publication, neither the author, neither publisher, nor the affiliates assume any responsibility for errors, omissions or contrary interpretation of the subject matter herein. Any perceived slights to any specific person(s) or organization(s) are purely unintentional.

We have no control over the nature, content and availability of the web sites listed in this book. The inclusion of any web site links does not necessarily imply a recommendation or endorse the views expressed within them. We take no responsibility for, and will not be liable for, the websites being temporarily unavailable or being removed from the internet.

The accuracy and completeness of information provided herein and opinions stated herein are not guaranteed or warranted to produce any particular results, and the advice and strategies, contained herein may not be suitable for every individual. Neither the author nor the publisher shall be liable for any loss incurred as a consequence of the use and application, directly or indirectly, of any information presented in this work. This publication is designed to provide information in regard to the subject matter covered.

Neither the author nor the publisher assume any responsibility for any errors or omissions, nor do they represent or warrant that the ideas, information, actions, plans, suggestions contained in this book is in all cases accurate. It is the reader's responsibility to find advice before putting anything written in this book into practice. The information in this book is not intended to serve as legal, medical, or accounting advice.

Foreword

This guidebook will discuss all of the things that you need to know in order to get started as an owner of a Greyhound. Bringing home a new addition for the first time can be a really exciting endeavor. The whole family may have spent time picking out the puppy that they wanted to bring home, and now they are excited to bond with him and to make some lasting memories.

This book is going to walk you through the steps that you need to follow in order to raise your Greyhound well, get your puppy trained and ready to behave.

Included inside this book's first section is about the origin and bio of a Greyhound. It contains the general information and the characteristics of this specific dog breed.

The Second section is about choosing a Greyhound. It tackles about where and how to acquire a Greyhound and how to select a healthy Greyhound dog.

The next section will talk about the things that you need and have to do as a Greyhound owner.

The fourth section focuses on how you can cater your dog's nutritional needs.

The next section delves into basic care and regular grooming needs for your Greyhound.

The sixth section is about raising and training your Greyhound. It educates dog owners about the importance of training and activities for your dog. It additionally contains a puppy's training outline and guidance in shaping behaviors, training, and problem solving.

Th seventh section focuses on the common health issues of a Greyhound and how to deal with them and respond into emergencies.

Chapter eight is about preparing your Greyhound for a dog show.

For the last section, it will talk about the breeding process for your Greyhound.

By obtaining this training guide, you will be on your way to securing the necessary tools and knowledge to assure your success as a Greyhound dog owner and trainer.

Table of Contents

Introduction 1

Chapter One: Greyhound Facts and Descriptions 3

    History 3

    The Athletic Runner 5

    As a House Dog 7

    Physical Characteristics 9

Chapter Two: Choosing and Acquiring a Greyhound 15

    Looking in All the Right Places 16

    The Reputable Breeder 16

        Breeder Advantages 17

        Breeder Disadvantages 18

    Greyhound Rescue Organizations 18

        What You'll Find from Rescue Groups 19

        Breed Rescue Advantages and Drawbacks 19

        Finding a Breed Rescue Group 21

        The Breed Rescue Process 21

    Animal Shelters and Humane Societies 22

        Types of Shelters 23

        Shelter Advantages and Drawbacks 24

    Selecting a Healthy Greyhound Puppy 25

What To Look For When Viewing A Litter And The Breeders Facilities 25

Viewing A Litter Of Puppies 26

Qualities To Be Aware Of When Choosing A Working Puppy 38

Choosing A Healthy Greyhound Puppy 38

Naming Your Puppy 40

Leaving His Mother And Litter Mates 41

Chapter Three: Preparing for Your Greyhound 43

Necessary Supplies and Equipment 43

Habitat Requirements For Greyhounds 44

Necessary Supplies And Equipment 46

Puppy Proofing Your Home 58

Introducing Your Greyhound To Other Family Members 63

Children 64

Other Pets 66

Chapter Four: Feeding Your Greyhound 71

Nutritional Requirements for Greyhound Dogs 72

Protein 72

Carbohydrate 73

Fats 73

Vitamins 74

    Minerals 74

    Water 74

How Much Food Should I Give My Dog? 75

How Frequently Should I Feed My Dog? 76

Chapter Five: Grooming Your Greyhound 79

    The Coat 80

    The Nails 80

    The Teeth 81

    The Ears 82

    Bathing 83

Chapter Six: Training and Behavior Modification 85

    Teaching Basic Commands 85

        Teaching Come 87

        Teaching Sit 87

        Teaching Down 88

        Teaching Stay 89

        Teaching Heel 90

    Potty Training Your Greyhound Dog 92

        Establish Her Living Area 92

        Establish the "Toilet" Area 93

    Positive Reinforcement 93

        Treats 96

- Types of Treats 97
- How and When to Treat.. 100
- Bribery vs. Reward Dog Treating 102

Collar/Harness & Leash Training 103
- A Word On The Hazards Of Using Collars In The Field 103
- Walking Equipment (Collar Or Harness And Leash). 103
- Putting The Collar Or Harness On 105
- Initial Walk.. 106
- Training Steps... 106

Clicker Training Your Greyhound Dog............................. 108
- How Do You Use A Clicker For Training?................... 111

Understanding Wagging and Barking............................... 114
- What Does the Wag Mean? 114
- What Does the Bark Mean? 116

Managing Behavioral Problems In Your Dog................... 122
- Aggression 125
- Barking and Whining 126
- Chewing 126
- Digging 127
- Jumping 127

Dealing with Separation Anxiety 128

What Causes Dog Separation Anxiety? 129

Typical Dog Separation Anxiety 130

Distinguishing Separation Anxiety from Other Problems 133

Helping Your Greyhound Cope While You're Away 136

Going To The Park 141

Other Dogs And Their Communication Signals 144

How Dogs Greet Each Other 145

How To Interact With Humans 148

Games 149

Chapter Seven: Vet Care for Your Greyhound 153

Choosing A Veterinarian 153

Why Vaccinate a Puppy? 155

Common Diseases and Viruses 157

Other Diseases and Viruses 161

Additional Vaccinations 171

When Is a Puppy Vaccinated? 171

Do You Need a Pet Insurance? 172

De-Worming 173

Healthy And Sick Dog 175

When Your Greyhound Eats Something They Shouldn't 177

Stress 179
Chapter Eight: Showing Your Greyhound 183
　　Transporting Your Dog 185
Chapter Nine: Breeding Your Greyhound 189
　　Choosing When To Breed 189
　　Breeding Process 191
　　Birthing Process 193
　　Understanding Various Stages Of Growth 197
Conclusion 203
Glossary of Terms 205
Index 211
Photo Credits 219
References 221

Introduction

One of the best decisions that you will ever make in your life time will be to bring home a puppy. Better still, would be if you decide to bring home a Greyhound! Dogs are man's best friend and they are said to help people lead happier lives. Not only will they spread joy but also teach their owners to love unconditionally.

Greyhounds are generally extremely smart and can take command quite effectively. But they will need a little training to help them utilize their smartness and be able to display their best behavior inside and outside the house.

Initially, training your Greyhound might seem like a daunting task but, trust me; it is much easier than you think it is. As was mentioned, it is easy to train a Greyhound as they take command easily and you will be able to train yours in no time at all!

In this book, we will look at the steps that you must adopt to raise and train your Greyhound. I hope you find it helpful.

Let us begin.

Introduction

Chapter One: Greyhound Facts and Descriptions

History

The Greyhounds certainly hold a long and prestigious historical background, starting out in the Middle East and North Africa. Despite living in these countries that have unstable and unforgiving weather conditions, the Greyhounds still managed to survive and even garnered the attention from other cultures. Their vast history even reaches as far as Greece since the ancient Greeks mentioned them in

Chapter One: Greyhound Facts and Descriptions

writings, included in artworks made by the Egyptians, praised highly by a poet from Rome, and even mentioned in the Bible. This just goes to show that the Greyhound is a great canine that exhibits their qualities throughout the centuries.

Years later, the Greyhounds managed to make their way to Europe during the notorious times of the Dark Ages. Even back then, these dogs were commended for their great skill and capability in hunting that there was a law that was passed so that the royal game reserves made it forbidden for anyone living within a 10-mile radius of the king's forests to even own a Greyhound. This was to ensure that the forests were kept preserved and ensure that the royalty held control of their property.

Even in England, the Greyhounds continued to become popular probably due to how popular coursing and racing was at the time. The explorers from Spain and even the colonists coming from Britain brought these dogs on their ships and then brought them to the United States where the breed developed further, coursing coyotes and jackrabbits on the plains.

The Greyhounds are considered to be one of the first breeds to make an appearance in the American dog shows. It was in 1885 when the American Kennel Club (AKC) officially recognized the breed and registered them in their records. A year later, the first official coursing race was conducted to pay

Chapter One: Greyhound Facts and Descriptions

homage to the great speed of the Greyhounds and the National Coursing Association was born from it during 1906. The Greyhounds are best known for their skill in racing and has become one of the most popular breeds in many states. However, racing Greyhounds has become a controversial sport since it left many dogs that are later to be abandoned, sold to markets and laboratories, and even euthanized, especially those who have lost an important race or those who don't have a good track performance.

Today, the Greyhound remains to be a well-coveted canine among dog owners and considered to be one of the gentle giant breeds in the canine world. They tend to be couch potatoes, so give him plenty of exercise if you're thinking of owning one.

The Athletic Runner

Even with just the mention of their name, you should probably get a picture of what the Greyhound looks like. This renowned canine has been mentioned in a number of literature pieces, shown in several artworks, and even featured in many TV shows and movies. Their build is what they're best known for, making it seem like these dogs were built for one thing – speed. With their long legs, narrow head,

Chapter One: Greyhound Facts and Descriptions

and a muscular body to boot, it's no wonder that the Greyhounds are considered as one of the fastest, if not the fastest dog in the world. This sprinter has riddled his image all over the worlds, may it be in books or in posters, and the breed still has a number of mysteries that we still don't know even after so many years.

Being one of the oldest dog breeds in the world, it is speculated that the Greyhounds came from Egypt and were considered as valuable assets throughout the years. Even the likes of Cleopatra, General Custer, and England's Queen Elizabeth the First were mesmerized by the qualities of the Greyhound. Even General Custer raced his Greyhounds before he set out on his trip to the Little Big Horn. And because of the benefaction of the Egyptian and British Queens in racing these dogs, Greyhound racing later was known to be the "Sports of Queens".

Putting aside their noble heritage, there is still a lot of things to love about the Greyhounds. Despite their tall and intimidating appearance, these dogs actually have a friendly disposition towards people and other dogs, but most especially displaying utmost loyalty and love towards their family. Compared to other big dog breeds, the Greyhound isn't the aggressive type, even towards strangers. However, they will bark if they sense someone approaching the household.

Chapter One: Greyhound Facts and Descriptions

With their history as racing dogs, you should know by now that the Greyhounds have a high energy capacity. That belief takes a turn though, since Greyhounds have a tendency to become couch potatoes and their favorite hobby is sleeping or just lying around the house. While they are runners, the Greyhounds are not built for long distance running as their daily walks will be enough for their exercise needs. But the Greyhounds also make as good jogging partners for those living an active lifestyle.

Having a strong prey drive, you need to know that your Greyhound needs to be leashed whenever you're outdoors so he just doesn't take off in pursuit of a small animal. While they can be a handful, these big and brawny dogs are one of the most affectionate breeds in the world and they enjoy a good pat on the head and a lot of belly rubs. If you've gotten your Greyhound from a dog shelter, a breeder or as a retiree from the racetrack, you'll grow to respect this breed from their long and prestigious history that many figures have given the Greyhounds.

As a House Dog

When you're thinking about the Greyhound as a housedog, you should know a lot of things first. Many

Chapter One: Greyhound Facts and Descriptions

Greyhounds come as retirees from the racetracks, usually left being abandoned, sold to labs for tests, and even euthanized if they don't do well in the racetrack or lose an important race. Today, Greyhound racing is considered as a barbaric sport since it leaves many dogs only to be left alone or even killed off. However, even if your Greyhound comes from the racetrack or as a puppy, they make as a wonderful addition to the family because of their sweet nature and even the race retirees can adapt quickly to life at home. Before you even look for a greyhound puppy, check out rescues or shelters for Greyhounds that need the love in their life replenished.

While they are big dogs, the Greyhounds still have a short coat, making them prone to the cold. Instead of letting them stay outdoors during the colder seasons, let them stay and sleep inside the house, also letting them wear a warm coat to keep them comfortable may it be during the snowy or rainy weather. Their short coat does shed and it makes them prone to scrapes and cuts if they're not careful.

The Greyhounds are friendly and affectionate by nature, even going so far as becoming friendly to strangers, but some prefer to be aloof. But even with their friendly nature, a Greyhound should never be let off the leash whenever you're outdoors as he may begin running after a small animal that triggers his prey drive. These are fast dogs that can easily outrun you, so better keep them on leash when

Chapter One: Greyhound Facts and Descriptions

you're out for walks and have high, sturdy fences to keep them contained in your yard.

While many people think that Greyhounds are high-energy and destructive dogs because of their racing background, they're actually laidback and relaxed, preferring to chill around the house and even sleeping for most of the day. When they're indoors, you don't have to worry since Greyhounds are quite inactive. In fact, the only thing that you have to worry about is your Greyhound stealing your spot on the couch or hogging your bed.

Muzzling the Greyhound is a common practice, especially for the big ones that are retired from the racetrack. This is because the Greyhounds have a tendency to nip or bite other dogs which can hurt the smaller dog breeds if the Greyhound's strong prey drive starts to take over. Muzzling the Greyhound until he gets used to things at home and you learn about their personality is recommended by a lot of people so that he doesn't injure you, your other dogs or himself.

Physical Characteristics

Greyhound has wonderful physical attributes, which makes it one of the fastest animals on land. Its long legs and

Chapter One: Greyhound Facts and Descriptions

arched back allows it to contract and stretch with minimum effort. While running, you will discover that the tail acts more like a rudder and a brake.

They also have longer legs, necks, less aesthetic muscles, bunched up, arched backs and deeper chests. Furthermore, their short and smooth coat comes in various colors namely liver, red, white, blue and black.

Size, Weight and Life Expectancy

Greyhound is the smallest in the family of gazehound, and weighs about 5- 15 lbs. They have a lifespan of 10- 15 years.

Coat Coloration

Greyhound is available in variety of colors namely black, seal, fawn, white, and sable. Blue and red are the most common colors of Greyhound. The coat is short, simple, fine and comes with a glossy shine.

Head and Neck

Greyhound has an elongated head and neck. The nose and eyes are usually round, medium-size and dark in color.

Chapter One: Greyhound Facts and Descriptions

His teeth are scissors-like. The ears are folded, small and delicate, while the arched neck is slender and long.

Body Structure

Greyhounds have a deep and narrow chest. The forelimbs are long, straight and lean. The hind limbs are well muscled, long and straight. The toes are highly curved, the tail is long and slender, and well curved, while the stifles or knee joints are well bent.

Temperament

Greyhound has an amazing temperament. They are always eager to please. Regarded by many as 'world's fastest couch potato'- it is reserved, timid, and can be sensitive among strangers. He is capable of chasing any small thing that moves quickly like cats and other domestic animals, and can relate well with other dogs and pets it has grown up with.

Greyhound has the following enviable characteristics:

- charming,
- loving,
- not particularly vigilant,
- not difficult to housebreak,
- laid-back,

Chapter One: Greyhound Facts and Descriptions

- gentle,
- intelligent,
- devoted,
- hardly bark,
- tremendous stamina,
- friendly,
- easygoing,
- calm and
- possess an aura of natural authority.

People are so happy with Greyhounds because of their wonderful temperament-non-aggressive and friendly nature-give them a little treat or reward, and they will likely be your friend for life.

Greyhounds are independent, intelligent and catlike in several ways. With mistreatment, they can easily become timid or shy, even if the mistreatment was unintentional.

Their temperament is affected by a wide range of factors, namely:

- socialization,
- training and
- heredity.

Greyhounds with nice temperament are usually playful and curious. Just like other kinds of dogs, Greyhounds need early socialization. You really need to

Chapter One: Greyhound Facts and Descriptions

expose them to varied experiences, sounds, sights and people while they are growing up. The socialization process will make him to be a well-rounded dog.

Enrolling him in a puppy kindergarten class would be one of the best things to do. Invite visitors to your house at intervals, take him to a walk, or to a busy parks or stores where he can meet other breeds- these activities will surely enhance his social skills.

Chapter One: Greyhound Facts and Descriptions

Chapter Two: Choosing and Acquiring a Greyhound

You've evaluated your lifestyle and come to the conclusion that you have the energy, time, and patience to live happily with a Greyhound. You know what activities you want to do with the dog, and you've studied the breed standard, so you understand what you're looking for in a Greyhound. Your children are sturdy enough to enjoy playing with a high-spirited Greyhound and old enough to take on simple dog care under supervision. All you have to do now is consider where to get the Greyhound of your dreams.

Chapter Two: Choosing and Acquiring a Greyhound

Looking in All the Right Places

When you're ready to get your Greyhound, you have a number of choices when it comes to deciding where to acquire your new dog. You can purchase a Greyhound from a breeder or adopt one from an animal shelter or a rescue group. Each source has advantages and disadvantages. Take a look at the options so you can make the choice that's right for you.

The Reputable Breeder

Anyone can breed two Greyhounds and sell the puppies. They don't have to know anything about dogs or have a license. Ideally, however, you'll buy your Greyhound from a hobby breeder (also referred to as a reputable or responsible breeder). This is someone who has been involved with Greyhounds for several years — showing their dogs in conformation classes, field trialing them, or participating in obedience trials.

This breeder should belong to the National Greyhound Association, as well as to local all-breed or specialty dog clubs. Hobby breeders study pedigrees carefully, looking to find the best matches for their dogs' strengths and weaknesses. Prior to breeding, they take their dogs to the veterinarian for health screenings to rule out such heritable

Chapter Two: Choosing and Acquiring a Greyhound

conditions as elbow or hip dysplasia, heart disease and eye problems.

Note: A good breeder can be the source for a first-rate Greyhound puppy or a well-adjusted older Greyhound that has retired from breeding or the show ring. It's your job to sort out breeders who are just out for a buck from the committed breeders who are dedicated to the breed's well-being.

Breeder Advantages

There are many advantages of purchasing from a reputable breeder. You can see the mother and every so often the father if he's in the same locale. (Females are frequently shipped long distances to be bred with the perfect male.) Although the father isn't in the area, the breeder may have videos or photos of him. You may also be able to see other relatives of the puppies you're planning to buy. This is important because it gives you a good idea of what your Greyhound will be like as an adult.

Breeders can also become mentors. They're there to answer questions as your Greyhound goes through adolescence — always a trying time — and if you want to show your dog, they can guide you through the process. If you live in the same location as the breeder, he or she may board your dog while you're not home or traveling, allowing

Chapter Two: Choosing and Acquiring a Greyhound

him to stay in a familiar place and giving you peace of mind that he's being taken care of. And if there's ever a reason you can't keep your Greyhound, a true reputable breeder will insist on taking the dog back to keep him or find another home for him.

Breeder Disadvantages

What are the disadvantages of purchasing from a reputable breeder? Sometimes they can be hard to find. It takes persistence and patience to find the one that's right for you. But then again if you want to get your money's worth, a hobby breeder is the way to go. You will know that your new pup has been raised in a home by a knowledgeable breeder, who has bred high-quality dogs and provided her pups with proper nutrition, veterinary care, and early socialization.

The main priority of a reputable breeder is that his or her puppies go to a decent home where they'll be loved all their lives. Be cautious of a breeder who pressures you to take one of his or her puppies or who seems apprehensive to get rid of puppies.

Greyhound Rescue Organizations

What if you want a Greyhound, but you like the idea of giving a home to a dog in need? A Greyhound rescue group can give you the best of both worlds. The National Greyhound Association, supports rescue efforts by maintaining a list of people nationwide who help place lost or abandoned Greyhounds.

What You'll Find from Rescue Groups

As with the Greyhounds found in shelters, these are usually dogs six months or older. Usually, before they're placed, they are spayed or neutered, checked for heartworm disease, vaccinated, and tattooed or microchipped. Sometimes the Greyhounds in rescue have behavior problems — such as fence jumping, digging, or barking — but the rescue group can help you find training to resolve the problem. Greyhounds adopted from breed rescue groups usually go on to become wonderful family companions.

Breed Rescue Advantages and Drawbacks

Adoption from a Greyhound rescue group has several advantages. Generally, people involved in breed rescue are committed to the welfare of the Greyhounds they work with and try hard to match people with the right dog. They follow up with new owners after the adoption, counseling and offering advice as needed.

Chapter Two: Choosing and Acquiring a Greyhound

Before you decide that breed rescue sounds like an inexpensive way to get a Greyhound, be aware of the disadvantages. Puppies are seldom available through breed rescue groups. This is true even with breeds, such as Greyhounds. People whose Greyhounds have puppies usually know that an ad in the newspaper will sell the puppies.

The National Greyhound Association, maintains a national emergency fund to help care for Greyhounds that are abandoned in multiple numbers after the shutdown of a puppy mill or that need help in the event of a natural disaster, such as a tornado or flood. It helps pay for immediate care needs, such as vaccinations, health checks, or short-term boarding.

Also, be aware that the heritage of a puppy or dog adopted through a breed rescue group is hardly known — and if it is, it's generally not of very high quality. Generally speaking, the people who surrender a Greyhound to a rescue program are not the people who have carefully selected a breeder. Furthermore, you don't have the benefit of being able to see the health clearances on the parents. Severe hip dysplasia or other hereditary or congenital problems may not appear for some time.

Chapter Two: Choosing and Acquiring a Greyhound

Finding a Breed Rescue Group

To find a Greyhound rescue group in your area, contact the National Greyhound Association. You can also go to your favorite search engine and type in "Greyhound breed rescue and [your state]." When you find a Greyhound rescue group, ask for literature on the program, such as a brochure or newsletter. Take a look at the adoption contract; it should state that the program will accept the return of the dog for any cause if you are unable to keep it. Another prerequisite should be that all dogs placed are spayed or neutered first, with exceptions only for age or medical conditions.

The Breed Rescue Process

Adopting from a breed-rescue group isn't as simple as going in, selecting the dog you want, and writing a check for it. Like reputable breeders, breed rescue volunteers are concerned in what you bring to a dog's life and care. They want to reside each dog in the best possible home, and this requires a period of evaluation that takes time. The wait is influenced by the number of other equally or sometimes more suitable applicants and number of dogs available.

Rescue programs differ in what they require for adoption. Some insist on a fenced yard (often with

Chapter Two: Choosing and Acquiring a Greyhound

prohibitions on electronic fences), as well as an appreciation of the amount of exercise a Greyhound needs. All look for a realistic lifestyle for good dog care. Expect to be asked whether you have time for a dog, which is understandable when you consider that a major reason Greyhounds are surrendered to rescue programs is a lack of time to maintain and exercise the dog properly.

You'll be requested to fill out an application first. Most groups require and check references, preferably from a veterinarian and a trainer. Many groups also schedule home visits, so they can evaluate the environment where the Greyhound will be living, as well as your experience with and readiness for Greyhound. Adoption fees typically range from $150 to $300. That's a pretty good deal, in view of what you get: a spayed or neutered dog with current vaccinations and a health check.

Honestly provide all the information requested by the rescue group about yourself and your home. Be willing to permit the home visit, and don't be upset by what may seem to be personal questions. Just as you want a good Greyhound, the rescue group wants good homes for its dogs.

Animal Shelters and Humane Societies

Chapter Two: Choosing and Acquiring a Greyhound

Believe it or not, you can find a nice Greyhound in an animal shelter or humane society. Sometimes, puppies are turned in to shelters when the persons that bred them hasn't been able to sell them. Other times, adolescent or older Greyhounds are given up because their caregivers decided they didn't have time for them. If you are considering getting an older Greyhound, or you like the idea of giving a home to a dog that really needs one, but there's not a Greyhound rescue group in your area, the shelter can be a good place to look. Expect to find Greyhounds between six and eighteen months of age, although there might be some that are younger or older.

Types of Shelters

No two animal shelters are identical, and there is no such thing as a centrally organized Society for the Prevention of Cruelty to Animals (SPCA) or humane society that oversees local organizations. You can look for a Greyhound at a municipal animal shelter — one that's funded by tax dollars and user fees. Municipal shelters implement animal control ordinances, license dogs, and quarantine animals that have recently bitten someone. They identify lost pets and return them to their owners when possible. Progressive municipal shelters with enough budgets may offer such services as community education, animal placement, and vaccination clinics.

Your city may also have one or more privately funded nonprofit animal shelters. There are so-called "no-kill" shelters in which they pick and choose which animals they'll accept, based on species, age, health, adoptability, and

Chapter Two: Choosing and Acquiring a Greyhound

availability of kennel space. Often these shelters send out newsletters or have Web sites listing the sorts of dogs they have available.

If your local shelter doesn't have any Greyhounds available, check out www.petfinder.com . Animal shelters and rescue groups post descriptions there of animals that need homes, and potential adopters can search the site by area, breed, and other parameters.

Shelter Advantages and Drawbacks

The greatest advantage of adopting a Greyhound from a shelter is that warm, fuzzy feeling you get from giving a needy dog a good home. Another benefit is the variety of services provided by some shelters. You may go home with a Greyhound that has been health-checked, spayed or neutered, and vaccinated. He may even know basic obedience skills or housetrained. Some shelters offer behavioral counseling and training classes so the two of you can get off to a good start.

The disadvantage — if you can call it that — adopting from a shelter is that most of them don't offer instant gratification. Like breeders and Greyhound rescue groups, many shelters nowadays have a rigorous screening process. They want to make sure that the dogs they place go to forever homes, not temporary housing. While it might seem difficult, think of it as a benefit to the dog rather than as a hoop you must jump through.

Sometimes, however, the only place to adopt a dog is an understaffed, overburdened city shelter. Be aware that

Chapter Two: Choosing and Acquiring a Greyhound

adopting from a shelter where the staff does not have the resources and time to evaluate each animal entails an element of risk. It's one thing to take home a Greyhound with an unknown history that has been evaluated by a trained shelter employee. It's quite another to take home a Greyhound without knowing anything at all about him. On the other hand, this risk can usually be overcome by working with a behaviorist or trainer after the adoption.

Selecting a Healthy Greyhound Puppy

Once you have sited at least one reputable breeder with puppies available, you will want to view the litter to hopefully select your Greyhound puppy. Before actually viewing the litter, it is important to observe and take note of the breeders' facilities.

Please note: It is important that when viewing a litter of puppies that they are at least 5 or 6 weeks of age, actively moving about on their feet.

What To Look For When Viewing A Litter And The Breeders Facilities

- Do the breeders' facilities as well as their home, appear clean, healthy and well maintained?

Chapter Two: Choosing and Acquiring a Greyhound

- Look for signs that the puppies live in the house such as a play pen, toys, food and water dishes, beds etc.
- Ask whether the puppies have started to receive house-training as well as other basic obedience.
- Find out to what extent the puppies have been socialized, with appliances, other animals, people of all ages etc. Do you notice evidence of this?
- Do they or other family members play interactive games with the puppies?
- How often has the breeder handled the puppies per day from the puppies first week of age?
- If the puppies are kenneled outside, is the facility clean (no feces or stale urine smells), dry, warm, fresh clean water available, chew toys etc.?
- Can the breeder offer a backup service if you need to ask questions or get advice?

Viewing A Litter Of Puppies

When initially viewing a litter, taking your children or someone with you can be useful to get different opinions, but try to keep an objective, impartial view yourself. Do not be swayed to pick a puppy for the wrong reasons. If you have the pick of a litter or at least a few, you are bound to be drawn

Chapter Two: Choosing and Acquiring a Greyhound

to one in particular. You ideally want a puppy who is friendly and approachable to you. The whole family will of course eventually need to be present when actually choosing a puppy.

If it is possible to spend at least an hour observing the puppies, you will see how they react to their normal surroundings. You are likely to see what they attempt to chew, and what they do when needing to do their toilet business. Again, an indication as to whether they have been toilet trained or not. If you can, watch the puppies being fed as well to make sure that they have a healthy appetite. A puppy that does not eat is likely to be sick.

The breeder may admit that the puppies have been contained in a large play area which has sheets of paper or some form of litter, allowing the puppies to toilet where they please. At least you will know that your toilet training will have to start with a similar arrangement, because that is exactly what they will do when they start living with you. If the puppy has been used to that arrangement up until 8 weeks you will have to be patient as it will take time for them to get used to your house-training routine.

The following assumes that you have the pick of the litter or at least more than one puppy. If not, then you may still be able to use most of the guidelines to determine the temperament of the puppy.

Chapter Two: Choosing and Acquiring a Greyhound

For this next part you are advised to have a note book and pen to take down notes of observations.

Observing The Litter At A Distance

Firstly, observe the litter from a distance without any interaction. Also try to view the pups in a confined area as well as running freely outside and notice if they react differently.

Observe how they interact with each other. Take note of their traits such as ones that are timid, boisterous, domineering etc., as such traits may be an indication of how the puppy may behave when older. Are they generally alert and curious, responding to what is going on around them? The more assertive or bossy types may be more difficult to manage and train, the more easy-going ones, less so.

- Notice the overall size of the puppies and whether some are larger than others
- Do they move with any apparent defects, limping, awkward gait etc.?
- Do you notice any discharges from their eyes, nose, anal area etc. The eyes and nose should look bright, clean and clear.
- Do you see any diarrhea or vomit in the play area?
- Notice whether they run up to you, run away, appear fearful, bark, attempt to play and interact,

Chapter Two: Choosing and Acquiring a Greyhound

dominant or bullying of litter mates, appear curious, confident etc.
- Are the puppies active, playful and lively or lethargic because they are ill or maybe they have just been fed?
- Ask whether the breeder has designated certain puppies as show and some as pet quality, and what are their reasons?

Interacting With The Litter

After the initial observations you should interact with the puppies. Ideally, the puppies' mother should be present and should be in good health and confident and friendly towards you, and certainly not hostile or wary. This is a very good indication of what the puppies will be like. Introduce yourself to her first then approach the puppies.
- Sit or kneel down to greet them as they will feel more at ease and more likely to approach you than if you are looming over them. Ideally, they should be confident and not shy with you.
- Spend a few minutes engaging with each puppy. Play with a toy to gauge the puppy's activity and try petting him to make sure he doesn't respond with fear or aggression.
- When you first make contact with the puppies, notice which one makes first contact and whether they stay close to you and interact. A 6- to 8-week-

Chapter Two: Choosing and Acquiring a Greyhound

old puppy will not have had chance to learn any polite etiquette when greeting you. So, expect them to gallop over to you, jump up or attempt to chew your hand. This is all quite natural, confident behavior and certainly not an indication of a future problematic, aggressive dog. A timid, shy, fearful puppy on the other hand may be a sign that insufficient socialization has taken place. Again, this is not the end of the world for a puppy. It just means that his 'rehabilitation' to bring him out of his shell will take longer than the confident puppy.

- Ask the breeders permission if you pick one up and only do so when you are sitting/kneeling close to the ground. Be very careful as some can wriggle and are easily dropped.
- You can usually calm him by gently stroking him along the ridge on the top of his head, between his eyes. You can also try gently massaging his ears, chest or around the jaw where it hinges.

Are they happy to let you handle them or again do they show fear, or attempt to wriggle and bite your hand? They should ideally be happy and relaxed and not wriggle too much. Try and handle all of the puppies and use this time to inspect the puppy. You will notice straight away whether a puppy is familiar with being handled once you attempt to pick one up. If they run away or struggle, then it is

Chapter Two: Choosing and Acquiring a Greyhound

likely that this aspect of their socialization has been neglected.

- Again, check their eyes and ears closely for traces of a discharge. The eyes should be clear and bright with no cloudy, opaque appearance. Certainly not inflamed or showing signs of discharge or weeping.
- The nose should look clean and bright, again with no discharge or dry crusty skin.
- The ears should be clean and free from any discharge. The puppy should have good hearing and be responsive and alert to sudden noises, which they may be shocked by, but show no signs of fear.
- There should be no signs of breathing difficulty such as wheezing or unusual panting and certainly no coughing.
- The mid-section should show no obvious rib protrusions, tummy or naval swelling.
- » Make sure there are no unusual lumps anywhere. Check that their paws look healthy and the pads are free from any cracks. The nails should not appear split and should be trimmed. Take a look in the puppies' mouths to see if it is pink and not pale. Being pink is indicative of a healthy mouth.

Chapter Two: Choosing and Acquiring a Greyhound

- The coat should look clean and soft with a pleasant odor. The fur should look groomed and un-matted. If you part the fur, there should be no signs of parasites or black specs indicating parasite feces.
- The skin should look healthy and be free of flaking, disease or inflamed lesions.
- The anus should not look inflamed or generally unclean. There should be no signs of stained hair possibly indicating a discharge.

Asking Questions About The Litter

Again, a note book and pen will come in handy. Have questions pre-written, for you to then write down the answers.

Has basic obedience taken place? You can quickly check whether the puppy has received any obedience training. Either issue the commands of sit, come, down etc., or ask the breeder to demonstrate these. Again, it's not the end of the world if they haven't, but it will be further indication of the good, reputable breeder you ideally want to deal with

Check that the parents have been health tested for hereditary diseases and ask for proof/certification now.
Have the puppies been wormed and vaccinated, if so when, or when will they be?

If you decide to take out insurance, can the breeder provide free temporary cover. Again, a reputable breeder

Chapter Two: Choosing and Acquiring a Greyhound

will be keen to have their own insurance cover whereas a puppy farm is less likely. You may be able to get free temporary cover anyway from a number of insurers, with no obligation to take out full cover with them.

Can the breeder offer a backup service if you need to ask questions or get advice? Will the breeder, for whatever reason, be prepared to take the puppy back? A lot of breeders actively engage in contracts with written guarantees to confirm their willingness to take back a puppy. Check what the contract implies, as certain breeders impose conditions such as not being permitted to breed from a bitch and so forth.

Temperament Testing

Opinions differ as to whether temperament testing a Greyhound puppy is a reliable indication of what a puppy will be like as an adult. It is up to you whether you wish to proceed with this when you greet the litter. It could be a valuable indication of what the puppy will be like as an adult. However, it could prove to be completely inaccurate.

Within a litter of puppies, there will exist many similarities that make each puppy have roughly the same characteristics. However, in the same way that children from the same family can have very different temperaments, so too will a litter of puppies. The individual puppies are likely to have different unique genetic combinations to each other. So, although they are all likely to look very similar or the

Chapter Two: Choosing and Acquiring a Greyhound

same, their personalities are likely to differ to varying degrees.

There are a number of temperament tests that you could perform that indicate whether a puppy is currently of a dominant or more compliant nature.

For example, when you pick up a puppy the more the puppy consistently struggles, bites, vocalizes could be an indication that a puppy has a dominant tendency. A normal puppy may struggle initially but calm down and accept the situation. A submissive puppy may not struggle at all, panic and appear fearful or even submissively urinate.

Tossing an object to gauge the puppy's reaction has a similar effect. The average puppy will chase, play with, return with the object if you call and allow you to take it. A submissive puppy is characteristically likely to shy away from the game, perhaps showing fear. The dominant puppy is likely to take the object away, perhaps jealously guard it with growls if you attempt to take it back. A puppy with a strong aptitude to retrieve should at least show an interest in going to pick an object up and carrying it, whether they return it to you or not.

Encourage a puppy to come to you, again by kneeling down, clapping your hands and softly calling the puppy. This will again elicit typical displays of dominance, submission or normal behavior. The dominant puppy will either ignore you or boldly charge at you. A submissive puppy again will either run and hide, or warily approach

Chapter Two: Choosing and Acquiring a Greyhound

you, perhaps rolling over onto their side. With normal behavior the puppy should confidently trot over to you showing no extremes of the other two.

It is debatable whether these behaviors continue into adulthood as a group of puppies may have had limited social contact, but will display either extreme. Shy puppies may be more timid and sensitive and if they remain so to a certain extent will no doubt suit a sensitive, quiet, thoughtful person. A gregarious, loud, brash sort of a person needing a bold guard dog will have an ideal dog in the dominant characteristic. The average person wishing to have an easy going, happy, confident dog would obviously be best suited to the normal, average temperament showing neither extreme.

For the purposes of a Greyhound, particularly as a working dog, the normal middle temperament would probably be the best choice. Shyness isn't a big concern as the puppy can easily develop into a very confident adult. A confident dog is ideal. The shy or dominant puppy may take longer to train. A dominant, independent nature is also not ideal for training, as the dog is less likely to obey commands.

Has Adequate Socialization Taken Place?

Socialization is extremely important during a puppies first 6 months, and equally so in the first 8 weeks. A reputable breeder will ensure the puppy has been exposed to everything going on around the house. This ensures that the

Chapter Two: Choosing and Acquiring a Greyhound

puppy has no fear of the similar sights, sounds and smells around your house. Even kennel bred puppies should be exposed to household experiences and therefore brought into the house a number of times per day.

Daily handling should have been started by the breeder and should continue once the puppy comes to your home. The handling should take place by as many different people as possible. Not only members of your family, but strangers also, who are likely to want to greet and pet a new puppy anyway. This handling should always be gentle and never rough. Children especially should be taught how to carefully and respectfully hold, pet and play with the puppy.

Handling should not just take place when a puppy is walking or running about. At the neonatal stage, a puppy is barely able to see, hear or walk. But they can feel and have a developed sense of smell. They are also at a sensitive and impressionable age. So being handled at this stage is very important and can do so much good.

In this respect, it is important to ask the breeder in a general sense, how the puppies have been socialized. They should hopefully say that they have been handled throughout their neonatal period. You should also hear that this has happened several times a day, every day, by adults, children and occasional strangers. It is worth asking, how many different people have been involved. As the puppies grow it is important that these interactions have included play time.

Chapter Two: Choosing and Acquiring a Greyhound

Regardless of what you are told, you will soon find out once you handle the puppy yourself. Whilst they are on all fours, gently hold and restrain them. As mentioned previously, they may struggle or wriggle a bit, but if the puppy shows signs of distress at this, they have probably not been handled very much, if at all.

You can also test how much socialization a dog has received by how quickly they recover from a sudden noise. Always ask the breeders permission before you attempt this, and explain what you are about to do.

If you clap your hands and a puppy recoil with fear and terror it is likely socialization has been relatively non-existent. You can also test by talking loudly, or make sudden laugh, shouting, crying, hissing, whistle sounds etc. Always have a food treat to hand to tempt the puppy back to you and for reassurance that you are friendly.

You ideally need to be sure that the puppy has been exposed to loud, sudden noises, shouting, screaming, crying, all domestic appliances, loud music, TV etc.

Under socialized dogs who react with fear in this way, as adults can compensate with aggression, which needs correcting with remedial rehabilitation. This usually involves gradually exposing an affected dog to the very thing they fear.

Chapter Two: Choosing and Acquiring a Greyhound

Qualities To Be Aware Of When Choosing A Working Puppy

Natural ability and trainability are traits that cannot really be taught, but bred into the dogs from proven generations displaying such traits. 'Pointing' is an obvious example. However, not all dogs are quiet and soft mouthed and hard mouths and vocalizing such as whining can be hereditary.

When viewing the litter are the parents relatively placid and easy to handle? It is important that the temperament of the dog is friendly and should certainly never show any kind of aggression to people or other dogs.

Are they relatively slow and steady or live wires? A dog that is too head strong, stubborn and independent is likely to be difficult to train and consequently difficult to control.

Choosing A Healthy Greyhound Puppy

Whilst you are spending this time interacting with the Greyhound puppies, you should be able to gauge which puppy is a good personality match for you. Hopefully, the preceding advice will have confirmed which puppy you will choose. Quite often you instinctively choose the puppy you like the look and personality of. If the Greyhound puppy

Chapter Two: Choosing and Acquiring a Greyhound

appears to be physically healthy and does not show any behavioral warning signs such as aggression, excessive fear, or lethargy, then he is probably a good buy.

You may at this stage decide this is the breeder you are happy with, choose your puppy and leave a deposit. If so, then it will be advisable to take care of a few preliminaries before the puppy finally comes to live with you:

Obtain a diet sheet or at least information regarding the diet the puppy has been weaned on and will be eating once he comes home with you. You will then need to check your local pet suppliers, unless the breeder can recommend one, to ensure you will be able to have this ready for the puppy's arrival.

If possible, visit the Greyhound puppy as often as you can so that they get used to you as a familiar person. Check to see if the breeder will allow you to leave an old blanket, 'vetbed' or other bedding that the puppy and litter mates can personalize. This will be comforting for the puppy as it will have the scent of his mother and litter mates when he comes to live with you.

It is also very important to check the Greyhound pup's inoculation status. In other words, has the puppy received any vaccination jabs as yet? If not then you need to contact your vet, giving the pups date of birth and to then start the

Chapter Two: Choosing and Acquiring a Greyhound

course of vaccinations as directed as soon as possible after you take ownership.

Ask the breeder about transferring Kennel Club ownership. If they haven't already done this, contact the Kennel Club and ask for the relevant forms to fill in and send them off.

Naming Your Puppy

Once you have finally chosen the Greyhound puppy you want, now will be a good time to decide on his name. You can then ask the breeder if they can start calling him by that name. Don't worry if this is not possible as dogs quickly get used to their name. This even applies to rescue dogs that already have a name, they soon get used to the new one. You probably already have ideas yourself, but if not, please make the name short and sweet. Something like, Daisy, Tess, Max or a name that relates to his appearance such as Patch.

Naming a dog is usually based on personal choice, but some names are more suitable than others. Short names of no more than two syllables make it easy to use when calling them. Be aware however that some names may sound similar to a cue/command word e.g., 'Stay' (similar to May, Jay, Jane etc.) 'Sit' (similar to Brittney or Brit, Kittie or Kit, Fitz etc.). It is not a big problem, but you do not want to confuse your dog

Chapter Two: Choosing and Acquiring a Greyhound

unnecessarily. It is also important to never use his name for anything negative or your dog will try his hardest not to respond when he hears it.

Leaving His Mother And Litter Mates

This is likely to be an anxious, confusing time and will not be an easy transition for a Greyhound puppy used to living with his mother and litter-mates, to then be suddenly separated without any warning. Which is why it is important to make this easier by providing him with familiar objects or scents whilst still with the litter.

Once he comes to live with you, another useful product that you may wish to consider, is known as DAP (Dog Appeasing Pheromone). DAP is a synthetic product based on the natural Pheromone the bitch gives off during birth which acts as a comforter to the pups. It is also effective for older dogs, again acting to comfort them and alleviate the stress of a new situation. These or similar devices usually plug into an electrical socket and diffuse the chemical in a similar way to an air freshener. If you use one, try and plug this in a day or so before the puppy arrives. Choose a part of the house where the puppy will sleep or spend most of their time resting. Pheromone is also useful for dogs that get anxious of certain events such as car journeys and if you can get this in spray form it is worth a try.

Chapter Two: Choosing and Acquiring a Greyhound

Chapter Three: Preparing for Your Greyhound

Necessary Supplies and Equipment

In this chapter, you will learn the basics about making a home for your Greyhound including tips for setting up his crate, other habitat requirements as well as an essential shopping list of all the initial supplies and basic accessories you will need.

Chapter Three: Preparing for Your Greyhound

Habitat Requirements For Greyhounds

Should You Keep You Greyhound In An Outside Kennel?

The Greyhound is a large-sized breed so it a great deal of space, and this breed will appreciate having room to run and play outdoors, if possible. The Greyhound has a single coat thus, it is not advisable to keep him in an outside kennel permanently. He would not certainly be tough enough to withstand relatively harsh temperatures, and, this is likely to be uncomfortable for him. Apart from that, being a sociable breed, he will not appreciate being separated from you, his family for long. This being the case, you should never keep your Greyhound outside for extended periods of time during the winter. On the opposite end of the spectrum, high temperatures can be dangerous for your dog as well. If you let your dog spend a lot of time in the yard during the summer, make sure that he has a shaded area to retreat to and plenty of fresh water at all times.

However, opinions do differ as to whether to keep your dog in your house or outside in a purpose-built kennel/compound. Some people do one or the other or a combination of both. Traditionally, many gundog handlers believed it essential to house Gundogs in an outside kennel. The argument is that the dog will be happier to see you, keener to work and to please you during training. Conversely,

Chapter Three: Preparing for Your Greyhound

the house dog who has seen you a lot more during the day and has perhaps become bored is likely to be less keen and enthusiastic. If the dog in question is naturally double coated i.e., soft downy under layer and thicker, courser top layer, living in an outside kennel is a feasible option.

If the dog predominantly lives as part of the household there will certainly be a greater bond between handler and dog. My personal preference is that the dog should ideally live as part of the family, but with the option of an outside kennel on the odd occasion that it may be needed. It will certainly be useful to train him, get him used to both situations, for the following reasons:

- If you go away on holiday, it will be less traumatic if the dog has been used to spending some time in kennels at some point.
- You may have to vacate the house for major building work etc., making it unsafe or impractical for the dog to be in the house.
- You may have a house party again making it unsafe and perhaps stressful for the dog to be in the house
- The dogs are in fresh air which is considered healthier than a stuffy, centrally heated house.

Chapter Three: Preparing for Your Greyhound

Necessary Supplies And Equipment

The following are the basic items you should ideally have, to help care for him on a daily basis.

IMPORTANT: Make sure you have all the equipment and accessories needed BEFORE the puppy arrives. Do not leave everything up until the last minute, adding unnecessary stress to your life.

A) Checklist For Initial Supplies And Equipment

- Food and water bowl
- Puppy food and treats
- Suitable size dog bed with bedding
- Puppy size collar or harness and lead
- Basic grooming equipment
- Assortment of soft toys and chew toys
- Flea treatment and wormer if the puppy has not recently received these. Also, ask your vet to recommend flea and worm treatments. Although these may seem more expensive than pet store brands, they are usually more effective. They can also advise you on a plan of treatment, which usually depends on the size and weight of the dog and dosage per kilogram etc.

Chapter Three: Preparing for Your Greyhound

- First aid kit
- Poop bags
- Sprays and deodorizers
- Stair/doorway baby gate
- Pet insurance
- Canine toothbrush and toothpaste (not immediately essential, but good to have on hand to use within the first 2 weeks or so. However, your local pet supply will no doubt be able to advise you on suitable products to buy to get you started)
- Crate (optional)
- Play pen (optional). Start by looking at items available at your local pet supply.

B) Initial Supplies

You will undoubtedly be busy spending as much time as possible with your new Greyhound puppy when he first comes home, so make sure you have prepared all the items he will need for his arrival.

Essential shopping list

You will be looking at one off items such as a crate and ongoing expenses such as food and pet insurance. The following will offer details from the previous list of essentials

Chapter Three: Preparing for Your Greyhound

to get you going. Most towns and cities have a good pet store where you should be able to get most if not all items needed. I personally would get your initial supply, certainly food, from the local pet store before you look at buying perhaps the same items cheaper online.

Bowls for food and water

Avoid plastic as these can easily scratch and harbor bacteria. Tough wearing stainless steel are considered the best choice as it is easy to clean and again does not harbor bacteria. However, even though ceramic has the risk of breakages they are a far healthier option to plastic. The weight of ceramic also makes it more difficult to overturn. It is possible to get non-slip stainless steel dishes, which seem like a good idea. Cheaper versions do seem to have a removable rubber ring, that although may not be as risky as plastic, still has the potential to harbor bacteria if not regularly cleaned. I personally prefer the dishes that have their own stand, elevated versions are easier for the dog to eat and drink. They are often recommended for dogs such as Whippets and Greyhounds who are at risk of gastric torsion.

Food

Chapter Three: Preparing for Your Greyhound

You should have been given a diet sheet or at least the information from the breeder with the type of food the puppy has been living on. Stick to that diet initially as changing the diet is likely to cause stomach upsets with the puppy.

Treats

Treats will be an important addition as it is advisable to use these for any positive reinforcement training, including early toilet training. Again, the breeder may have been offering treats, but if not, I suggest asking the advice of your local store as to a good quality food treat that they supply. Certainly, do not be tempted with the cheapest you can find. However, my own preference is to make them yourself. It is easy to buy a block or cheese or corned beef for example. Cut them into small cubes of no more than 1 cm square, spread them on a tray and freeze. Once frozen you can then put them in a freezer bag and take out a handful or so for a training session. You could also search the internet or YouTube for [homemade dog treats] to get more ideas. Again, treats are advisable as a training aid, so it is likely you will be using a lot initially. Try to ensure that as well as being nutritious, the treats help to exercise gums and clean the teeth.

Suitable size dog bed with bedding

Chapter Three: Preparing for Your Greyhound

A soft donut type bed is a good idea, for him to snuggle into. Many breeders and dog owners also recommend a 'vetbed' type product for possible accidents. You don't have to buy the most expensive or luxurious, but make sure it is a reasonably good quality that will withstand regular washes. Washing the bedding can be done once a month or sooner depending on the extent that the puppy is bringing dirt in on its coat. Again, go with recommendations from pet stores but it is advisable to not get a dog bed much larger than half their eventual size. You will then need to purchase another suitable for their adult size in several months' time.

Again, there are many more choices from hard plastic bucket types to all soft padded base and sides. It is probably more important the choice of bedding, whether you use an old blanket or duvet or again, buy sheets of 'Vetbed', or similar product. When you are house-training your puppy, it is certainly best to use an old blanket or a towel, just in case your puppy has an accident. Once your puppy is fully trained, however, you can upgrade to a plush dog bed or a thicker blanket that will be more comfortable. Many people choose to use a temporary box whether cardboard or otherwise and then a proper bed when they are nearing their full-grown size in a few months' time. The other consideration with a choice of bed is the issue of the puppy chewing anything and everything. In this respect beanbags,

Chapter Three: Preparing for Your Greyhound

foam and wicker baskets can potentially be destroyed in no time. If you opt for a crate, to make it more comfortable, you should line it with a soft blanket or a plush dog bed. You may also wish to purchase a specific crate mat, many of which are water and chew proof.

Lead and collar

A specific puppy lead and collar is recommended initially. But these do not have to be of a high quality or expensive. A young puppy is hardly likely to have the strength to break the cheapest collar or leash. But remember that as they grow you will have to replace them for their adult size. Flat collars are obviously better than traditional choke chains which can cause damage to the neck and throat whilst an over exuberant puppy is first getting used to them. Flat collars can be either leather or nylon webbing and preferably the wider the better again to alleviate any potential force to the throat area. Traditional Greyhound collars are often recommended for young puppies as they are much wider and more comfortable than standard flat collars.

Depending on the law for your area, ID tags with your name and address may be a legal requirement, whereby this should be clearly displayed and attached to the collar if the dog is taken into a public place.

Chapter Three: Preparing for Your Greyhound

Grooming

The grooming requirements for a young Greyhound puppy are likely to be different to that of an adult dog. All puppies have relatively soft coats and so a soft brush or similar will be sufficient initially. Nail clipping is also something that many dogs do not like, so getting them used to this as early as possible is highly recommended. This again will be covered in the chapter on grooming. However, as a rule, only the very tip of the nail should be taken off, if necessary. It is important that you know how to do this, as it is easy to cut the 'quick' of the nail and make it bleed.

Grooming Supplies

The following will give you some indication as to what you will need in grooming. Grooming a Greyhound is simply a matter of a quick brush once or twice per week. The grooming tools you are likely to need to brush and bathe your Greyhound at home include:

- Bristle brush
- Hound glove
- Rubber mitt
- Trigger spray bottle

Chapter Three: Preparing for Your Greyhound

- Shampoo and conditioner
- Tooth brush and toothpaste
- Nail clippers
- Ear drops
- Cotton wool
- Dry towel
- Hair drier
- Optional flea comb
- Optional grooming table

Toys

These include toys that you interact with your Greyhound dog, such as for retrieving, tug toys etc., Kong type toys to stuff with food for added interest, general chew toys and puzzle toys offering mental stimulation.

Chew toys

Chewing is an important and natural activity for dogs at any age and serves a number of very useful purposes. For the young puppy, chewing can relieve the discomfort of teething. At any age the act of chewing releases endorphins, which in turn has a calming effect. Dogs will also chew to cope with boredom or frustration, as well as symptoms associated with separation anxiety. With a wide variety of chew toys, it is a very important alternative to floss teeth and exercise gums in the absence of raw meaty bones. They also hopefully provide a distraction and an alternative if you accidentally leave shoes lying around that you would prefer to keep intact. More seriously they provide an alternative to chewing electrical cables which can obviously be dangerous, potentially causing a fire risk, and fatal to the dog if the cables are live. Different dogs, like different toys, so your best bet is to buy several different kinds and let your dog choose which ones he likes best.

First aid kit

It is advisable to familiarize yourself with general first aid awareness and in some cases, this may be necessary to save your dog's life. First aid kits are obviously useful for anything that does not require veterinary attention. You can of course make up a first aid kit yourself. I would however, recommend buying one from your local pet supply initially.

Poop bags

Consideration for pedestrians and other dog owners means that any feces need to be picked up and properly

Chapter Three: Preparing for Your Greyhound

disposed of. Many local authorities insist on this and non-compliance can lead to a sizeable fine. You can buy disposable poop bags, but do consider cheaper options such as disposable nappy bags for babies or other bags, which are biodegradable.

Sprays and deodorizers

Accidents can and will happen but make sure that the product you use is safe for a dog to be exposed to. A good natural alternative spray cleaner/deodorizer is vinegar. Although obviously not a cleaning agent, an anti-chew spray can be effective in keeping a puppy away from items that they may find attractive to chew, but are difficult or impractical to remove from a room, such as part of a wooden chair or other furniture.

Stair/doorway baby gate

Simply restricting your Greyhound puppy access to a room or part of the house is far easier than trying to train him to keep out. The foot of a stairway is an obvious area that could be hazardous for a puppy to climb. Baby gates are also useful if you need to keep the puppy temporarily confined to one room. They also enable the puppy to see what is going on, rather than having the door shut. This will not make the puppy feel so isolated.

Pet insurance

If you are debating whether it is worth taking out insurance, I would at least seriously consider it whilst the puppy is relatively young. There is no easy option with pet insurance and it really is a question of researching what cover your dog gets for the price you pay. Local insurance companies are a good place to start as are internet comparison sites, as well as recommendations from friends or your vet.

Crate

A crate basically offers a dog a den for them to rest in, safe confinement when travelling by car and a safe place for them to reside when you cannot supervise them. If you use it correctly your Greyhound dog will not view time spent in the crate as punishment and there is no reason to believe that keeping your dog in a crate for short periods of time is cruel. If you use the crate properly while training your Greyhound, he will come to view it as a place to call his own. He will soon see it as place where he can go to take a nap or to get some time to himself if he wants it. This of course assumes that you

Chapter Three: Preparing for Your Greyhound

leave the door open or remove it. Covering the crate is also a good idea as it makes it darker and more secluded, which many dogs like.

When selecting a crate for your Greyhound, size is very important. For the purpose of house training, you want to make sure that the crate is not too big. It should be just large enough for your puppy to stand, sit, lie down, and turn around comfortably. Dogs have a natural aversion to soiling their dens. If your puppy's crate is only large enough for him to sleep in, it will be more effective as a house-training tool. When your puppy grows up you can upgrade to a larger crate. The following dimensions are considered to be a good general size for a Greyhound: 48" L x 30" W x 32.5" H. As crates can be expensive, you may wish to choose one that will be suitable for the size they will be as an adult. Obviously from a financial point of view, you really do not want to be buying a small size for now, then a medium or large etc.

Puppy pen

Once again, a puppy pen is a great idea to give them freedom to romp but to also stay out of harm's way. These can be set up indoors or outside in the garden/yard. Your local pet supply should have examples to give you an idea of the size and price.

Chapter Three: Preparing for Your Greyhound

Puppy Proofing Your Home

Puppy proofing your home is a good way to ensure you and your Greyhound get off to a good start together. Otherwise, he could cheerfully destroy your house while he investigates it. Puppies, especially Greyhounds, are smart little guys, and they are very curious about everything.

It is important to puppy-proof your home to prevent that destruction before your Greyhound comes home. To properly puppy-proof your home, follow the tips below.

Put up Any Hazardous Items

Pick up and lock away any items that can be hazardous to your Greyhound. These include:

1. Household cleaners
2. Vitamins
3. Medication
4. Vehicle fluids, such as antifreeze
5. Salts for ice or water softener
6. Pool / lawn chemicals
7. Tobacco products
8.

Chapter Three: Preparing for Your Greyhound

Puppy's Eye View

Take the time to crawl around your home before your Greyhound puppy arrives and then once or twice a week. Look at things from your puppy's vantage point. Pick up small clips, tags, paper, anything that can be a choking hazard for the puppy.

Also, keep clothes picked up. It can be surprising, but some articles of clothing, such as socks, can pose a choking hazard for your Greyhound.

Put Knick-Knacks up High

While you may love having your ornaments on tables and shelves, look at what your Greyhound can reach. If he can get it, move it up out of reach. Wagging tails have a way of knocking things off balance.

Puppies also like to explore by putting things in their mouths. Putting your objects away will prevent the item from being broken and your puppy from getting hurt. It does not have to be permanent but only until your Greyhound learns what he is and is not allowed to touch.

Close Off Access to Standing Water

Chapter Three: Preparing for Your Greyhound

Close toilet seat lids, drain tubs and sinks and block off any access to a pool if you have one. Standing water can be very tempting for an Greyhound. However, young puppies cannot swim, and falling into the water could lead to drowning.

Tie Up Those Electrical Cords and Drapery Cords

Electrical cords are always very tempting for a puppy and are often chewed. Always tape your cords out of reach of your puppy. Also, look for cords that dangle from furniture as they may knock a clampdown on themselves while playing with a cord. Do not forget about the computer and phone cords. Make sure they are tucked away if possible.

In addition to electrical cords, pull up the drape or blind cords. These can lead to strangulation if the puppy gets caught in them.

Keep Garbage Out of Reach or in a Puppy Proof Container

Another tempting item for puppies is the garbage can. Always keep it put up where the puppy can't get at it, and make sure you empty it every night, especially if your puppy isn't sleeping in his crate. Bathroom garbage cans are a great source of interest and contain a good deal of hazards like

Chapter Three: Preparing for Your Greyhound

discarded razors, q-tips, cotton balls, etc. It is ideal to have trash cans with a lid to minimize the chance of investigation by curious puppies.

Block Off Stairs

Even if you allow your Greyhound upstairs with you, block off the stairs at both the top and the bottom. Puppies do not have a lot of coordination, and taking stairs can be difficult for them. It is quite common for a puppy to fall downstairs. To prevent this, keep the stairs blocked and off-limits.

Keep Doors Closed

Any door or window leading to the outside should be kept closed if the puppy can access it. An open door can be irresistible for a puppy.

Check the Outdoors

Also, to puppy-proof your house, make sure that you check the outdoors. Look for openings in the fence and items that can be hazardous to your Greyhound puppy. If there are any drain pipes, pools, or other items in your yard, they can present a risk. If you find anything, pick up all the hazardous items and fence or block off the rest, such as the pool or drainpipes. The goal is to make the outdoors as safe as indoors.

Look at Your Plants

Finally, look at the plants that you have in your home and garden. Many plants are poisonous to dogs, so avoid having them in your home. If you do have them, make sure they are in areas where your puppy cannot reach them.

In the end, puppy-proofing is simply keeping your house neat and tidy—and taking a few precautions. Everyone in the home should work with you to keep the space clean, and you should constantly reassess if your house is still safe for your Greyhound puppy.

The Right Spot

"Outside" is probably not a specific enough spot for you for his evacuation. You probably don't want him to think of your whole yard as his toilet, especially if you have kids. So be consistent and take him to the exact spot you want him to use. Once there, give him a specific one-word command. He'll quickly learn to head to the right spot at this command.

Chapter Three: Preparing for Your Greyhound

Choose another simple command to use when you want him to relieve himself. This will help him remember what to do, and you'll find it helpful when you are out and about and need to instruct him to use a new place away from home—so pick a word you won't be embarrassed to use in public! "Get busy" or "Do your business" or are good choices.

Introducing Your Greyhound To Other Family Members

Once your Greyhound puppy is home, it is time to introduce him to the other residents in your home. While your first instinct is probably to rush in and introduce him to everyone, your Greyhound can become very frightened or overwhelmed by too much attention all at once. A puppy can withdraw and shut down if he is overwhelmed by his surroundings or by meeting too many people.

Since you want all introductions to be positive, it is best to make the introductions as calmly as possible. Let your puppy have time to get used to his new home.

One of the best things that you can do for your puppy when you bring him home is to allow him to rest in a quiet room. After he has had some time to adjust, start bringing in people to meet him, one at a time.

Chapter Three: Preparing for Your Greyhound

Other animals in the home can wait a day or two. There is no rush and you want to do the introductions properly to prevent any lasting problems for your Greyhound.

Children

For younger children, it is a good idea to introduce them to your Greyhound puppy one at a time. This will help minimize the amount of stimulation the puppy has. If you have older children, you can introduce them together.

When you are introducing your Greyhound puppy to children, start by having your child come into the room and sit down on the floor. Do not rush the puppy or place the puppy in your child's lap. Instead, give the child treats to feed the puppy and allow the puppy to approach on his terms. Tell the child to stay calm and quiet so the puppy won't get frightened. Greyhounds have a natural fondness for children so your puppy should gravitate to the child. When the puppy does greet the child, let the child pet the Greyhound calmly. Keep meetings short and build up their length. Besides, over the first few days, make all interactions with the children calm and quiet. As the puppy gets used to the sounds of children, you can start introducing playtimes.

Chapter Three: Preparing for Your Greyhound

It is important that children should have rules regarding the puppy, and they should be taught how to treat the dog.

Make sure your children understand the following rules:

a) Be calm around the puppy.
b) Don't hold onto him when he wants to go.
c) Never hit or pinch the puppy.
d) Don't pull on ears or tail.
e) Gently pet the puppy.
f) Use toys to play with the puppy.
g) Don't try to take toys or food away from a puppy or dog.
h) Don't run away from a puppy or dog.

Unfortunately, most puppies and dogs do not respect children the same way they do the adult (taller) members of the family. Your children won't be able to command your puppy with the same authority that you have until they are a little older. It is important that an adult is always present to supervise when small children play with puppies and dogs to keep accidents from happening. Once your children are a little older, your dog will respect them more, and play is less likely to get out of hand. As you train your Greyhound puppy, you should include your children in the puppy's training and socialization. This will be helpful for both your puppy and your children in the long run.

Other Pets

Introducing your Greyhound puppy to other pets in the home is something that you should do gradually. Remember that the animals in the home were there first and they can have some behavioral issues with a new puppy such as jealousy or problems with the territory.

To prevent these issues, make sure you make the meetings short and that you do not force any relationships. The animals in your home will sort out their hierarchy on their own.

When introducing other pets, it is important to follow these rules:

Keep Your Puppy Confined

The first rule is that you should always keep your puppy confined when you bring him home. Place your Greyhound in a quiet room. This will keep your puppy safe while still making your current pet feel confident.

When you are bringing the puppy out of his room, confine the current dog unless you are taking the time to introduce them.

Chapter Three: Preparing for Your Greyhound

Allow Door Sniffing

Or crate sniffing. What this means is that you should allow your current pet to sniff at the crate or the door where the puppy is. Don't let them be pushy and if your puppy starts to look stressed, stop the behavior.

Sniffing at the door will help your pet become acquainted with the puppy while there is a safe barrier between the pet and the puppy.

Set Up The Meeting

Plan meetings between your current pet and your puppy in advance. Never bring in a puppy and then allow your current pet to take charge. Instead, wait until your current pet is calm before you make the introductions. This will help promote a positive experience for both your new Greyhound and your current pet.

Encourage Your Current Pet To Equate Your Puppy With Positives

When you are doing the introductions, always provide your current pet with plenty of affection. Give him lots of praise for greeting nicely and make sure that you give him plenty of treats. The more you praise your current pet, the more he will think the new Greyhound puppy is something positive.

Let Cats Greet On Their Terms

While you can control the meetings between a dog and a puppy, it can be difficult to control the meeting between a puppy and a cat. Often, puppies find cats interesting (too interesting) and will try to chase the cat or play with him. When this happens, the cat will usually react.

Make The Older Pet The Primary Pet

What this means is that your current pet should have more rights than the puppy. The current pet should be fed first, you should greet him first when you get home, and you should always allow the current pet to enter or exit first.

Be Patient

Finally, be patient with your pets. Remember that this is a big adjustment for them and that they may not warm up quickly.

Chapter Three: Preparing for Your Greyhound

Many times it can take up to 6 months for the puppy to be accepted by the current pets. For cats, it can take up to a year.

Chapter Three: Preparing for Your Greyhound

Chapter Four: Feeding Your Greyhound

Feeding your Greyhound a healthy diet is the key to maintaining his health and well-being. If you do not feed your Greyhound a high-quality food he could suffer from nutritional deficiencies as well as other health problems. Skimping on cheap dog food is false economy that could lead to health problems down the line and potentially expensive to treat. In this chapter you will learn the basics about dog nutrition and receive tips for feeding your Greyhound.

Chapter Four: Feeding Your Greyhound

Nutritional Requirements for Greyhound Dogs

Just like all living things, dogs require a balance of nutrients in their diet to remain in good health. These nutrients include protein, carbohydrate, fats, vitamins, minerals, and water. Dogs are a carnivorous species by nature so meat plays an important role in their diet, but they do require some carbohydrates as well. Below you will find an overview of the nutritional needs for dogs in regard to each of the main nutrients. Keep these nutritional requirements in mind when selecting a dog food formula for your Greyhound.

Protein

This nutrient is composed of amino acids and it is essential for the growth and development of tissues, cells, organs, and enzymes in your dog's body. Protein can be obtained from both animal and plant-based sources, but animal-based proteins are the most biologically valuable for your dog. There are two categories of amino acids; essential and non-essential. Non-essential amino acids are those that your dog's body is capable of producing and essential amino acids are those he must get from his diet. The most important essential amino acids for a dog include lysine, arginine, phenylalanine, histidine, methionine, valine, leucine, threonine, and isoleucine.

Chapter Four: Feeding Your Greyhound

Carbohydrate

The main role of carbohydrates in your dog's diet is to provide energy and dietary fiber. Dogs do not have a minimum carbohydrate requirement but they do need a certain amount of glucose to fuel essential organs like the brain. A dog's body is only capable of digesting certain kinds of carbohydrate and too much fiber in the diet is not good for them. The best types of fiber for a dog are moderately fermentable fibers such as beet pulp, cooked brown rice, and bran.

Fats

This is the most highly concentrated form of energy so it is an important part of your dog's diet. Fats provide your dog with twice the energy of protein and carbohydrates. Fats are also important for providing structure for cells and for producing certain types of hormones. They are also necessary to ensure that your dog's body can absorb fat-soluble vitamins. Your dog needs a balance of omega-3 and omega-6 fatty acids in his body and it is best if these fats come from animal-based sources instead of plant-based sources. Some of the best oils for dogs include salmon oil, general fish oil, cod liver oil, canola oil, and flaxseed oil.

Chapter Four: Feeding Your Greyhound

Vitamins

Your dog's body is incapable of producing most vitamins, so it is essential that he get them through his diet. Some of the most important vitamins for dogs include vitamin A, vitamin D, vitamin E and vitamin C.

Minerals

Minerals are a type of inorganic compound that cannot by synthesized and thus must come from your dog's diet. The most important minerals for dogs include calcium, phosphorus, potassium, sodium, copper, zinc, and iron. Minerals are particularly important for developing and maintaining strong bones and teeth. Vitamins and minerals can be purchased and administered as a supplement with instruction from your veterinarian.

Water

Water is the most vital nutrient for all animals. Your dog would be able to survive for a while without food if he had to, but he would only last a few days without water. Water accounts for as much as 70% of your dog's body-weight and even a 10% decrease in your dog's body water levels can

Chapter Four: Feeding Your Greyhound

be very dangerous. Provide your Greyhound with plenty of fresh water at all times.

How Much Food Should I Give My Dog?

Many people will respond in a variety of ways depending on their experience with their pets. However, the scientific facts regarding feeding elements in the case of dogs must be emphasized throughout the feeding activities maintained in the case of dogs.

Generally, pups should not be separated before the age of eight weeks. However, orphaned puppies do exist on occasion. Typically, 5% of the puppy's body weight is used as the criterion for the amount of food to be provided to the puppies. However, the quantity ingested by the dog varies with the size of the dog.

However, a good rule of thumb is to feed the puppy until you notice evident fullness of the abdomen to a modest degree. If you continue to feed the animal without paying attention to the look of the animal's stomach, the puppy may have digestive disturbances and diarrhea.

This may be quite inconvenient for both the owner and the dog. Puppies, as opposed to adult dogs, require less amounts of food but more often. However, as children get older, the amount may be raised to some level, but the frequency of feeding is frequently reduced.

A raw-diet dog may ingest only two to four percent of their body weight. Simply pay close attention to the dog's dietary routine and bodily condition. If the dog gets chubby, just lower the amount of food, and if the dog becomes lean, increase the feeding items.

As previously stated, puppies and teenage dogs consume more food than adult dogs. Similarly, due to the dog's diminished mobility, the elderly dog consumes less than the mature dog. However, when feeding the food to the elderly dogs, keep in mind to limit the quantity of protein.

How Frequently Should I Feed My Dog?

This is a frequently asked question by many dog enthusiasts and dog owners. If the puppy is under the age of six weeks, milk should be given five to seven times per day. If the puppy wants to eat, it will make some noise.

When the puppy is six to eight weeks old, the feeding frequency may be lessened. When the puppy reaches the age of four weeks, it may begin eating solid food. As a result, mix the solid food with water in the majority of cases and feed your puppy once or twice at first. If the dog suffers diarrhea, postpone the meal.

Most of the time, it is due to trial and error, but there are some essential processes in feeding that you should be aware of. After the age of eight weeks, the feeding frequency can be reduced to two to three times each day. However, if the dog is perceived to be hungry and in need of food, then feed food more often than the projected number of times. This varies depending on the breed of dog.

However, in this age range of dogs, avoid feeding too frequently. The puppy will be teething between the ages of three and six months. As a result, limit feeding to two times per day, but offer a balanced kind of nourishment to dogs of this age range to avoid deficiency-related problems.

Try using commercial puppy food between the ages of six months and one year. However, from the first year forward, adult food can be introduced gradually. However, as the dog ages, the frequency of feeding should be reduced since the movements of such mature dogs are greatly reduced for a variety of reasons. The pregnant animal, on the other hand, may be fed an extended period depending on the animal's willingness and restrict the quantity of food without sacrificing the quality of food.

Chapter Four: Feeding Your Greyhound

Chapter Five: Grooming Your Greyhound

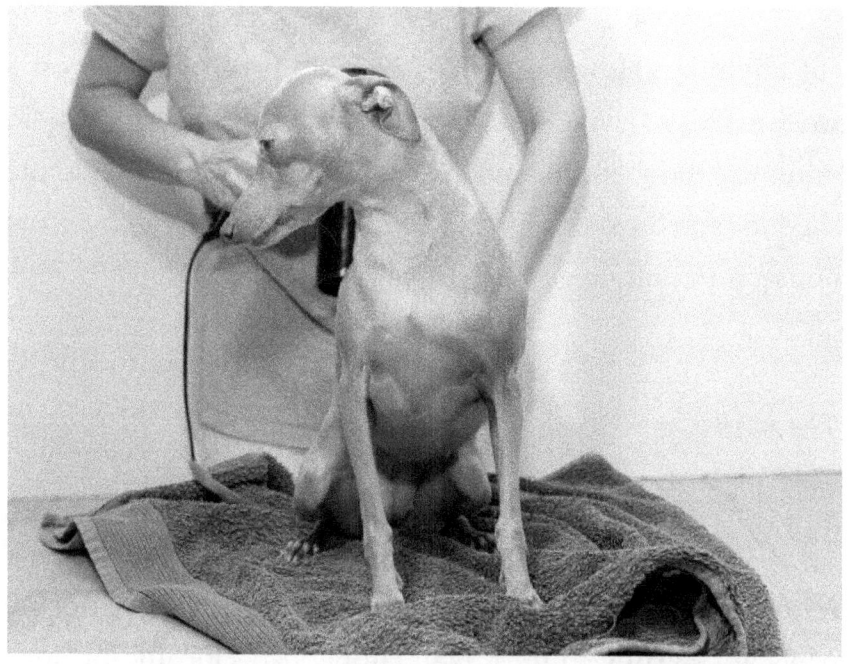

Greyhounds have short coats – which makes grooming them easier compared to long coated dogs. However, that does not mean that you can skip the grooming process entirely. Due to the unique features of the dog, forgetting to groom them in a proper way can easily lead to complications or infections that may rack up your veterinary bills. With just a few minutes of your time each day however, you can be sure that the Greyhound will avoid these problems.

Chapter Five: Grooming Your Greyhound

The Coat

The coat is short and soft so there's really no need to cut anything. However, you'll want to brush the coat on a routine basis, even just a few minutes each day just to minimize the shedding in your home. The breed is a moderate shedder so you shouldn't see much hair littering all over the house, especially if you groom properly.

The Nails

Trimming the Greyhound's nail should be done on a routine basis – every time you feel as though the little doggie paws are starting to hurt. Nail clippers specifically for dogs are best – but some dog owners actually get away with using nail clippers for humans. Either way, the clipper that has a one sure stroke will do. Using a buffer or a grinder instead of a clipper would also work as this tends to dull the ends of the nail. If you are going to use human nail clippers, make sure you follow through with a buffer.

What's important to remember when trimming your Greyhound's nails is not to go overboard with the trim. Check out the nails and you'll see a bit of whitish hue that starts from

Chapter Five: Grooming Your Greyhound

the root and ends halfway through the nails. You should NEVER trim past this since this is painful for the dog and could actually cause bleeding. Instead, cut just a few millimeters of the nail – just enough to dull the edge so that it doesn't wound your dog when he starts to scratch himself. This would also help prevent damage to the furniture or the carpet since some Greyhounds like to scratch in place.

Perhaps the hardest part about trimming a Greyhound's nail is the dog itself. Many dogs do not like having their paws held and will fight you when you try to clip their nails. This can be terribly difficult not to mention dangerous since you might clip a huge part of the nails. Proper training is important in order to properly trim a dog's nails.

The Teeth

Teeth grooming can be done in a variety of ways. The typical method is by simply brushing your dog's teeth using a special kind of toothbrush. This type of toothbrush has a smaller head and a longer handle, allowing you to reach the back teeth of the dog. Some dog owners get away with using a kid's toothbrush since the head is just the right size for the Greyhound's mouth.

Chapter Five: Grooming Your Greyhound

There's also the option of giving the Greyhound a toy that doubles as a toothbrush. These toys are made of certain ingredients that help clean the teeth so that the Greyhound's mouth is not just fresh but also sufficiently dulled.

Dry dog food is also a good way of keeping the dog's teeth clean. Unlike wet food that tends to stick to the gums, dry dog food doesn't have that 'stickiness' factor, allowing the dog's teeth to be mostly free from debris.

Again, teeth cleaning can be difficult since many dogs don't like to have their mouth touched. It's also unlikely that they'd stand still with their mouths open voluntarily. This requires a bit of training on the part of the dog owner.

The Ears

A dog's ears always need to be checked and often cleaned out. There many solutions on the market to loosen wax and make it easier to clean ears out. If you are in doubt ask the vet and if a dog's ears are blistered or red and sore looking ask the owner to take the dog to their vet where they can be sedated to have the proper, deep-down cleaning done and maybe antibiotics prescribed for infection.

Putting some ear cleaning solution into the ear and massaging lightly from the outside is the normal way to loosen wax. Then use cottonwool to take out the loosened wax

Chapter Five: Grooming Your Greyhound

and finish off gently with cotton buds. Some people use forceps to do this but gentle use of cotton wool should suffice.

Bathing

Greyhounds need to be bathed only as needed, and never more than once a week if it can be helped. Due to their small size, the Greyhound can be bathed in the kitchen sink, and with proper training, there should be very little fuss on the part of the dog.

Puppies are best bathed using lukewarm water and immediately dried after the wash. The use of a hair dryer should help, but please use only the lowest heat setting. Do NOT let the Greyhound swim around in a pool or the beach in lieu of bathing. They're generally not very good swimmers.

Chapter Five: Grooming Your Greyhound

Chapter Six: Training and Behavior Modification

Teaching Basic Commands

As a Greyhound dog owner, you want a calm and obedient dog. You want the relaxed and faithful type of dog. If you have a well-trained and obedient dog you will have less hassles and more comfort when you take your dog out with you. If you want to train your Greyhound dog yourself, you must use basic commands to train your dog.

Chapter Six: Training and Behavior Modification

Greyhound dogs are smart breeds of dogs. These dogs are loyal, versatile and are easy to train. Training a Greyhound puppy to learn basic commands is relatively easy compared to other dog breeds, as the Greyhound easily grasps the command training concept. If you put in a little dedication and are consistent, your Greyhound puppy will be trained in basic commands in minimal time.

If you minimize the number of mistakes and continually reward the positive behavior, your Greyhound will successfully be trained in basic commands. This training requires your full attention and commitment until your Greyhound puppy is fully trained to understand the basic commands.

Training your Greyhound dog properly is a great way to create an obedient dog, and also it will help the dog become a good companion and friend. Effective training will increase the bond between you and your dog and it will also strengthen your relationship.

To successfully train your Greyhound to obey your commands it's important to establish yourself as the pack leader. Greyhounds are pack animals and must follow a strong lead, much like humans. As the pack leader you need to maintain the power and control.

Chapter Six: Training and Behavior Modification

Effective dog training starts with learning basic commands like Come, Sit, Down, Stay, Heel. You must first get your Greyhound's attention in order to teach him anything. After all, he can't learn anything if he's looking at another direction with his mind focused on something else.

Teaching Come

This is the easiest command to teach your Greyhound, and you can start that training very early in his life. Call your Greyhound puppy over to you. You can say the dog's name and add, "come." When the dog responds correctly reward him with a food treat and praise lavishly. Gradually increase the distance between you and the puppy and be consistent in the practice to really reinforce the cue.

Teaching Sit

Once you have the dog's attention, have the treat in your right hand and the leash in your left. Place your right hand with the treat at the dog's nose and allow him to lick the treat but don't let him take it from you. Tell him to "Sit" and gradually raise your right hand from in front of his nose up over his head. This will have him looking at the ceiling.

With his head bent upward, his knees would have to bend to maintain his balance. With his knees bent, he would

Chapter Six: Training and Behavior Modification

assume a sit position. Now, let him have the treat and praise him profusely with comments like Good sit!, "Good dog!," etc.

Keep in mind that you must always praise lavishly, because Greyhounds, like all dogs, enjoy been praised by their owners or handlers and feel proud of themselves when they accomplish a behavior.

It is not necessary to use food forever in getting your Greyhound to obey your commands. Using food is only to teach new behaviors, and as soon as the dog understands your request when you give a specific command, the food treats will not be needed, but you will still use the verbal praise.

Teaching Down

Teaching your Greyhound the down exercise is easy. But it is important that you first understand how the dog perceives the down position. It is also important that you apply it correctly because using the wrong approach can sometimes make the dog react in a negative or undesirable way.

Get your Greyhound to sit close alongside your left leg, both of you facing in the same direction. Hold the food treat in your right hand and the leash in your left.

Chapter Six: Training and Behavior Modification

Next, place your left hand on the top of the dog's shoulders, but do not push down on his shoulders. Now allow your left hand to rest there making it easy to guide the dog to lie down near your left leg. Place your right hand at the dog's nose, and in a soft voice say "Down" and gradually lower your right hand to your Greyhound's front feet.

Once your right hand reaches the floor, start moving it forward in front of the dog. Continue talking to the dog in a soft voice, saying things like, "Do you want to eat this food treat? You can surely do this, good dog." The dog will follow your right hand so as to get the treat.

Once the dog's elbows are on the floor, let him have the food and praise him in a soft voice. Try to get your Greyhound to stay at that down position for a few seconds before you allow him sit up again. What you want to accomplish here is to get Greyhound to settle down and feel comfortable in the down position rather than feeling threatened.

Teaching Stay

It is easy to teach your Greyhound to stay in either a down or sit or position. Like before, food and praise can be used during the process to help the dog understand exactly what it is that is expected of him.

Chapter Six: Training and Behavior Modification

To teach your Greyhound the sit-stay, get the dog to sit on your left side. Hold the food treat in your right hand and have the leash in your left. Place your right hand at the dog's nose. Next, say, "Stay" and stand directly in front of your Greyhound (by stepping out on your right foot), toe to toe, while he licks on the food treat.

Make sure his head is facing upward so that he maintains the sit position. Now count to five and swing around to stand next to your Greyhound again with him on your left this time. Once you return to the original position, let him have the food treat and praise lavishly.

To teach your Greyhound the down-stay, do the down as described. Once your Greyhound assumes the down position, say "Stay" and just like before, step out on your right foot. Count to five and stand beside the dog with him staying on your left side. Let him have the food treat and praise lavishly again.

Teaching Heel

Heeling means that your Greyhound walks beside you without pulling. This will take time and patience on your part to succeed at teaching your Greyhound that you will not proceed unless he is walking calmly beside you. Pulling out his ahead on the leash is not acceptable.

Chapter Six: Training and Behavior Modification

Start by having the leash in your left hand while the dog is sitting beside your left leg. Grab the loop end of the leash with your right hand while keeping your left hand short on the leash, keeping Greyhound close to you.

Next, say "Heel" and then move forward on your left foot. Make sure Greyhound is close to you and then take three steps.

Now stop and get Greyhound to sit next to you - this is now called the heel position. Remember to praise verbally, but do not touch your Greyhound. Wait a moment and start again with "Heel." Take three steps and stop, and at this point tell the dog to sit again. What you want to accomplish here is to have Greyhound walk those three steps and not pull on the leash.

Once he calmly takes three steps beside you without pulling, take five steps this time. When your Greyhound will walk politely beside you as you take those five steps, try and increase it to ten steps this time. Keep increasing the number of steps you take until your Greyhound will walk calmly beside you without pulling.

When you want him to stop heeling, let the dog know that the practice is over. You can do this by verbally praising him and saying something like "Okay, good dog."

Chapter Six: Training and Behavior Modification

Potty Training Your Greyhound Dog

For you to house train an untrained Greyhound dog, you will probably need more time than if you are training a puppy. Nonetheless, commitment, vigilance, consistency, and patience is what will earn you success. Also, ensure you establish a routine as puppies perform better on a regular schedule. This method is based on time to eat, to play and to "eliminate" or use the potty. Most puppies or dogs can control their bladder for an hour for every month of age. Thus, 4 months old puppy can manage 3-4 hours.

Establish Her Living Area

Begin by deciding your Greyhound dog's living area, probably in a crate, kitchen, garage, or bathroom.

Try to spend some time with your dog in his or her living area, playing with him or her and feeding at the same spot. If he or she eliminates in the living area, you might withdraw a few treats or reduce your attention for him or her to learn that such behavior is unacceptable.

Chapter Six: Training and Behavior Modification

Establish the "Toilet" Area

Decide a place where the Greyhound dog goes to eliminate every time he or she gets the urge. You might need to accompany him or her to the potty area until he or she is accustomed to the routine. Below are some tips to help with potty training.

- It is important to establish a regular feeding routine so that you can learn the proper time when the dog eliminates.
- Don't confine the dog in the crate for too long to avoid him or her soiling the living area. Also, take him or her out frequently, at least every 2 hours, and again after waking up, eating, drinking or after playtime.
- While, at the potty, you can use a command such as "go potty" for the dog to be aware of what he or she would do after taking him or her out. After a successful potty routine, take him or her out for a walk or use other treats or praises.
- You can pick the water dish from the crate 2-3 hours before bedtime to minimize the probability that your dog will have to eliminate at night.

Positive Reinforcement

Chapter Six: Training and Behavior Modification

It is always better to reward your Greyhound instead of punishing him or her. Here are a few reasons why:

- If you punish your dog, it can make him distrust or cause fear, aggression, and avoidance of you. If you rub your dog's nose his doodie or pee, he may avoid going to the bathroom in front of you. This is going to make his public life difficult.
- Physical punishment has the tendency to escalate in severity. If you get your dog's attention by a light tap on the nose, he will soon get used to that and ignore it. Shortly the contact will become more and more violent. As we know, violence is not the answer.
- Punishing your dog may have some bad side effects. For example, if you are using a pinch collar, it may tighten when he encounters other dogs. Dogs are very smart, but they are not always logical. When your dog encounters another dog, the pinching of the collar may lead him to think that the other dog is the reason for the pinch. Pinch collars have been linked to the reinforcement of aggressive behaviors between dogs.
- Electric fences will make him avoid the yard.
- Choke collars can cause injuries to a dog's throat as well as cause back and neck misalignment.

Chapter Six: Training and Behavior Modification

- You may inadvertently develop an adversarial relationship with your dog if you punish your dog instead of working through a reward system and correctly leading. If you only look for the mistakes within your dog, this is all you will begin to see. In your mind, you will see a problem dog. In your dog's mind, he will see anger and distrust.
- You ultimately want to shape your dog's incorrect actions into acceptable actions. By punishing your dog, he will learn only to avoid punishment. He is not learning to change the behavior you want to be changed; instead, he learns to be sneaky or to do the very minimum to avoid being punished. Your dog can become withdrawn and seemingly inactive. Permanent psychological damage can be done if a dog lives in fear of punishment.
- If you punish rather than reward, neither you nor your dog will be having a very good time. It will be a constant, sometimes painful struggle. If you have children, they will not be able to participate in a punishment-based training process because it is too difficult and truly not fun.
- Simply put, if you train your dog using rewards, you and your dog will have a much better time and relationship. Rely on rewards to change his behavior by using treats, toys, playing, petting,

Chapter Six: Training and Behavior Modification

affection, or anything else you know your dog likes. If your dog is doing something that you do not like, replace the habit with another by teaching your dog to do something different, and then reward him or her for doing the replacement action, and then you can all enjoy the outcome.

-

Treats

You are training your Greyhound puppy, and it is going well because your pup is the best dog in the world. Oh yes, he is; everyone knows this to be true. Because of this fact, you want to make sure that you are giving your dog the right type of treats.

Treats are easy, as long as you stay away from the things that aren't good for dogs, such as; avocados, onions, garlic, coffee, tea, caffeinated drinks, grapes, raisins, macadamia nuts, peaches, plums, pits, seeds, persimmons, and chocolates.

Dog owners can make treats from many different foods. Treats should always be sized about the dimension of a kernel of corn. This makes them easy to grab from treat pouches and still flavorful enough for your hound to desire them.

Chapter Six: Training and Behavior Modification

All a dog needs are a little taste to keep them interested. The kernel size is something that is swiftly eaten and swallowed, thus not distracting from the training session. A treat is only to provide a quick taste, used for enticement and reinforcement, not as a snack or meal.

When you are outdoors, and there are many distractions, treats should be of a higher quality that is coveted by your pooch. Trainers call it a higher value treat because it is worthy of your dog breaking away from the activity they are engaged in. Perhaps cubes of cheese, dried, or cooked meats will qualify as your dog's high-value treat.

Make sure you mix up the types of treats by keeping a variety of them available. Nothing is worse during training than when your puppy turns his nose up at a treat because he has grown bored of it or it happens to be of lesser value than his interests hold.

Types of Treats

Human foods that are safe for dogs include most fruits and veggies, cut-up meats that are raw or cooked, yogurt, peanut butter, kibble, and whatever else you discover that your dogs like, but be sure that it is good for them, in particular their digestive system. Be guided that not all human foods are good for dogs. Please read about human

Chapter Six: Training and Behavior Modification

foods that are acceptable for dogs and observe your dog's stools when introducing new ideas for treats.

How many times have you heard a friend or family member tell you about some crazy food that their dog loves? Dogs do love a massive variety of foods; unfortunately, not all of the foods that they think they want to eat are good for them. Dog treating is not rocket science, but it does take a little research, common sense, and paying attention to how your dog reacts after wolfing down a treat.

Several people like to make homemade treats, and that is okay. Just keep to the rules we just mentioned and watch what you are adding while having fun in the kitchen. Remember to research and read the list of vegetables that dogs can and cannot eat, and understand that pits and seeds can cause choking and intestinal issues, such as dreaded doggy flatulence. When preparing, first remove any seeds and pits, and clean all fruits and veggies before slicing them into doggie size treats.

Before purchasing treats, look at the ingredients on the treat packaging, and be sure there are no chemicals, fillers, additives, colors, and things that are unhealthy. Some human foods that are tasty to us might not be so tasty to your dog, and he will let you know. Almost all dogs love some type of raw or cooked meat. In tiny nibble sizes, these treats work

Chapter Six: Training and Behavior Modification

great at directing their attention where you want it focused. Here are some treat ideas:

- Whole grain cereals, such as cheerios without sugar added are a good choice.
- Kibble (dry foods). Put some in a paper bag and boost the aroma factor by tossing in some bacon or another meat product. Dogs are all about those delectable smell sensations.
- Beef jerky that has no heavy seasoning or pepper added.
- Apple pieces, carrots, and some dogs even enjoy melons.
- Meats that have been cubed and are not highly processed or salted are easy to make at home as well. You can use cooked left-over foods.
- String cheese, shredded cheese, or cubed cheese; dogs love cheese!
- Cream cheese, peanut butter, or spray cheese, give your dog a small dollop to lick for every proper behavior. These work well when training puppies to ring a bell to go outside for evacuation.
- Ice cubes, but if your dog has dental problems, proceed vigilantly.
- Baby food meat products certainly don't look yummy to us, but dogs adore them.

Chapter Six: Training and Behavior Modification

- Commercial dog treats, but be cautious; there are loads of them on the market. Look for those that do not have preservatives, by-products, or artificial colors. Additionally, take into consideration the country of origin.

Never feed or treat your four-legged friend from the dining table because you do not want to teach that begging actions are acceptable. When treating, give treats far from the dinner table or from areas that people normally gather to eat, such as by the BBQ.

How and When to Treat

The best time to issue dog treats is between meals. Treating close to mealtimes makes all treats less effective, so remember this when planning your training sessions. If during training you need to refocus your dog back into the training session, keep a high-value treat in reserve.

Apparently, if your dog is full from mealtime, he will be less expected to want a treat reward than if a bit hungry. If your dog is not hungry, your training sessions will likely be more difficult and far less effective. This is why it is a good idea to reward correct actions with praise, play, or toys and not to rely exclusively on treats.

Chapter Six: Training and Behavior Modification

- Love and attention are considered rewards and are certainly positive reinforcement that can be just as effective as an edible treat. Dog treating is contained of praise, attention and edibles. Allowing some quality time or engaging in play with their favorite rope toy is also effective. At times, these treats are crucial to dog training.
- Do not give your dog a treat without asking for action first. Say, "sit," and after your dog complies, deliver the treat. This strengthens your training and their obedience.
- Avoid treating your dog when he is overstimulated and running amuck in an unfocused state of mind. This can be counterproductive and might reinforce a negative behavior resulting in the inability to get your dog's attention.
- Due to their keen sense of smell, they will know long before you could ever know that there is a tasty snack nearby, but keep it out of sight. Issue your command and wait for your dog to obey before presenting the reward. Remember, when dog treating, it is important to be patient and loving, but it is equally important not to give the treat until your dog obeys.
- Some dogs have a natural gentleness and always take from your hand gently, while other dogs need

some guidance to achieve this. If your dog is a bit rough during treat grabbing, go ahead and train the command "gentle!" when giving treats. Be firm from this point forward. Do not give treats unless they are gently taken from your hand. Remain steadfast with your decision to implement this, and soon your pup will comply if he wants the tasty treat.

Bribery vs. Reward Dog Treating

Bribery is the act of offering the food visually in advance so that the dog will act out a command or alter behavior. The reward is giving your dog his favorite toy, treat, love, or affection after he has performed the commanded action.

An example of bribery would happen when you want your Greyhound to come, and before you call your dog, you hold a cube of steak for them to see. The reward would be giving your dog the steak after they have obeyed the come command. Never show the treats before issuing commands.

Bribed dogs learn to comply with your wishes only when they see food. The rewarded dog realizes that they only receive treats after performing the desired actions. This also

Chapter Six: Training and Behavior Modification

assists by introducing non-food items as prizes when training and treating.

Collar/Harness & Leash Training

A Word On The Hazards Of Using Collars In The Field

It is extremely important that when out in a field environment where there is cover such as hedges, collars of any type should never be worn by your dog, puppy or adult. A Greyhound dog can very easily pass through hedges and get snagged quite severely and sometimes with fatal consequences. Chord choke type leads are always recommended for this purpose. The choke lead, being all in one, simply passes on and off the dog as required.

Walking Equipment (Collar Or Harness And Leash)

Dog walking equipment should be introduced carefully, particularly to a puppy, and only the kindest collars or harness types should be used.

A harness is generally better than a collar, as it redistributes the weight of his body and naturally, immediately stops him pulling on the leash.

Chapter Six: Training and Behavior Modification

Dogs are far easier to control on walks when wearing a harness and there is no nasty pulling and coughing, as often happens on a standard collar and leash.

If you intend to use a collar however, initially use a small leather or man-made collar suitable for a puppy.

When you put his puppy collar on, do make sure that it is not too tight. You should quite easily be able to slip two fingers under the collar. It is up to you whether or not you allow him to wear the collar around the house on a daily basis. Please however remember that he will be growing day by day so it is important to check that you can still slip two fingers under the collar, every other day.

Most puppies do not like having to wear a collar, but this is something you should apply within a few days of his arrival.

In the early stages, he will do everything to get the collar off. So simply accept that this is not cruel and wait for the scratching and head shaking etc to stop once he gets used to it.

Basically, when you first introduce a Greyhound puppy, or older dog, to a collar or harness make it a nice and positive event. Pop it onto the dog and play for a while, then remove it again whilst the dog is still happy. After doing this

Chapter Six: Training and Behavior Modification

a few times, add the leash and allow the dog to trail it behind in the house or garden.

Putting The Collar Or Harness On

As with any new training you can always sweeten the experience with a treat.

- Some people simply put the collar on and leave the puppy to get used to wearing it for an hour or so.
- Or if you prefer, you can do this in 5- or 10-minute stages by first putting the collar on > offering a treat > leave him five or ten minutes > take it off and repeat several times.
- Remember to give him lots of praise whilst he is accepting the collar, but ignore any protestations
- You can then take it off and leave him a few minutes so that he knows the collar is no longer on.
- You then put the collar back on, once again offer a treat, but this time leave him with the collar on for an hour or so.
- You next attach the leash to the collar and allow him to wander around with the lead trailing.
- Again, leaving this on for 30 minutes to an hour, so that he gets used to it.

Chapter Six: Training and Behavior Modification

- All of this should be done supervised as it could be dangerous for the pup if the lead in particular gets caught and potentially cause a choking.
- Once your puppy seems happy wearing the collar and leash, he should be ready to go for a walk.

Initial Walk

Obviously, we are not training the puppy to walk, but introducing him to the restriction imposed by applying the collar or harness and leash.

The following training steps are to help you prevent pulling on the leash. They are simply to make your Greyhound walking experiences happy and relaxed forever.

The steps may take longer if the dog has learned to grab the leash in his mouth or fight against the tension, but if you persevere, they will still work.

You will have more success with this if you start the training with few if any distractions. It is therefore best to utilize your yard, garden or a large room.

Training Steps

1. With your dog on his leash, walk a couple of steps and if the leash stays slack say 'good boy/girl' > offer lots of

Chapter Six: Training and Behavior Modification

praise and a treat. Please note that a slack leash is what we want and it is only that which should be rewarded.

2. If the leash becomes tight at any point, do not acknowledge this by speaking or offering any kind of reward. He needs to realize and associate that when he pulls on the leash, he does not receive a reward.
3. If the leash goes tight you may need to change direction a few times to initiate a slack leash. If your puppy does not follow immediately you may have to stop and call him by saying 'this way' or using his name, perhaps slapping your thigh as you do. I also find that by simply stopping, thus breaking the sequence of him pulling, is often enough to make him realize he shouldn't pull. Try and avoid suddenly stopping without him realizing and yanking him to a stop. Give him chance to stop, by calling him.
4. As soon as any tension vanishes from the leash, again say 'good boy/girl' > offer lots of praise and a treat. In other words, we are 'marking' the desired behavior with praise and a treat.

Be patient with this and please don't get into the habit that some 'impatient people' seem to do, and pull the poor dog back with enough force to pull him over. The dog is keen and excited to be out walking and sniffing about. Given the

Chapter Six: Training and Behavior Modification

chance he wants to go off and do his own thing. So again, please be patient and considerate.

Repeat and practice this several times, rewarding a slack leash each time. You should soon notice he gets into the habit of not pulling, but instead walking nicely.

Teaching a Greyhound to walk easily on a leash will probably take 3 to 6 training sessions in a quiet area. It will then need practice (proofing) in various areas, gradually increasing distractions, to become flawless behavior. This will eventually require exposure to roads and busy traffic. You will need to get to a point of teaching him to sit and wait at the road side until it is safe to cross.

Clicker Training Your Greyhound Dog

Clicker training is another method to train your Greyhound dog using positive reinforcement. Also referred to as mark and reward training, this training method involves using a clicker to condition your pooch to act in the ways that you want. After you associate it with a treat or reward repeatedly, the clicker becomes a conditioned reinforcer for your dog. Clicker training is similar to the positive reinforcement method, which we just discussed earlier. A clicker is just an effective noisemaker that makes training

Chapter Six: Training and Behavior Modification

more seamless for your dog. Clicker training tends to work more effectively with dogs because it tells them the exact behavior or action you are rewarding. It works more precisely. When you click at the right time, it marks the precise moment your dog responded to your command. So, rather than having your dog guess if he got it right or not, the noise from the clicker tells your pet precisely what he did right. This makes it easier for him to master and repeat the behavior. For example, if you are teaching your Greyhound to sit, you click at the time his butt hits the ground. This way, he understands that you are rewarding him for that specific action.

Think of the clicker as a tool for marking a moment, because that is precisely what it is. However, the clicker isn't effective in itself because it is meaningless unless you pair it with a reward. The click is simply an indicator that a reward is coming. In clicker training, rewards can be edible treats or basically anything the canine values. So, if you think your pup would prefer a game with his toy than a chunk of meaty stuff, then that should be your reward to him. The key is to time yourself correctly and be consistent. The click should mark the exact moment your pup does what you want and should always be followed with a reward.

You might be wondering how exactly clicker training works. In positive reinforcement, you reward a dog after he

Chapter Six: Training and Behavior Modification

performs a desired action or behavior. Without the use of a clicker, your dog might not know what he is being rewarded for. Clicker training helps with timing, and that is why it sometimes works more effectively than regular training with word of mouth. For example, when you are training your pooch to sit, you have to make it clear that you are rewarding his butt on the ground. Therefore, you have to make sure you give the reward while he is sitting down rather than when he stands up back. Clicker training is even more helpful if your pup is the type that stands back up as soon as his butt touches the ground. You can't get the reward to him fast enough, but he will be able to tell that the click is because of him sitting down. And then, you can give him the treat as a reward. The click marks the precise moment you are rewarding, bridges the gap until the reward gets to your dog, and helps ensure that your dog understands the action was done correctly.

Of course, you can use praise the same way, but it's usually not as clear to the dog. Most times, we communicate to our dogs all the time using praise as an indicator. That is an incredible way of rewarding your canine companion. But praise is not usually specific to training, and that is why it may confuse. Using a clicker or another training-specific instrument helps eradicate any confusion that might occur about the reward to come. Apart from the clarity it offers, clicker-trained dogs tend to learn faster. They are genuinely

Chapter Six: Training and Behavior Modification

interested in training and are willing to work hard to get a click. From your pet's perspective, mark and reward make training seem like a game, a fun game. It also takes the pressure off you – looking for moments to mark means you can focus on good choices made by your animal, instead of the mistakes. Mark and reward training enhance communication and makes training as lively as it can get.

How Do You Use A Clicker For Training?

To use a clicker for training, you must first teach your pooch what the marker represents. Do this by pairing the clicker with a reward. So, click, and then reward your pet immediately. After 10 to 20 practices, your dog will come to understand that the click sound indicates that a reward is on the way. After this, you can start using the clicker for your dog training.

Clicker training can be combined with the lure-and-reward training where you use a treat to lure your Greyhound dog to perform the action you want. But you can also use it to shape your dog's behavior. Shaping a dog's behavior is more difficult because it is like building something complex with gradual steps. It requires more time, effort, and patience on your part. The clicker also helps with capturing great behavior outside of training sessions. So, if you catch your dog "going" outside instead of soiling his bed, click and then

Chapter Six: Training and Behavior Modification

reward that behavior. Or, if the doorbell rings, you can click before you open the door. This will tell your pet to remain in one place instead of jumping in guests. Click training can also be used for teaching your dog new tricks. Eventually, when your pet has learned a new behavior with the use of a clicker, you won't need it anymore. It is merely a training tool.

I recommend using the clicker training technique if you have never trained a dog. Below is an example of how to get your pet to start associating the sound of the clicker with an on-the-way reward.

1. Fill a bowl with an assortment of treats. Make sure they all smell pleasant and appealing to your dog. They should be stuff that he likes.
2. Sit comfortably on the floor with the bowl within your reach, but out of your dog's reach. Hold one of the treats in your hand and the clicker in the other.
3. Click the clicker, and when your dog comes closer to investigate or his ears twitch, reward him with the treat. At first, he won't understand the reason or even care about it – it will be all about getting another treat from the bowl.
4. Repeat step 3 over and over. Click first, then treat. Click, treat. Click, treat. Always ensure he swallows one treat before you repeat the click-treat.

Chapter Six: Training and Behavior Modification

5. Soon, he will come to look at your treat hand whenever the click sounds. Good. That means he has realized that there is a connection between the click and the treat.
6. Once he understands that the click means a treat is coming, you can start using the click to point out the action you want him to perform and then reward him. For instance, you tell him to sit, wait till his butt plops on the ground, and click-treat immediately.
7. Don't worry if your pup looks confused. He simply wants to figure out where the click is coming from. When he sits again, click-treat, after 4 to 5 repeats, he will figure out that his behavior is what will get him the treat.

You may not know it, but dogs understand cause and effect. He will come to realize that his action is what is making you click-treat. Before long, your furry friend will start doing all you want to get you to make a click and give him a treat. He will believe that he can make you into his treat dispenser by doing the things you want. A puppy trained with clicker spends his time trying to please his master so he can be rewarded for his behavior. Be careful not to use the clicker when there is no reward at hand for your pup.

Chapter Six: Training and Behavior Modification

Understanding Wagging and Barking

What Does the Wag Mean?

It can be a mistake to just assume that if a Greyhound is wagging its tail that they are friendly and happy.

When determining a dog's true intent or demeanor, it's important to take into consideration the entire dog, rather than just the tail, because it is entirely possible that a dog can be wagging its tail just before it decides to take an aggressive lunge toward you.

More important in determining the emotional state of a dog is the height or positioning of its tail.

For instance, a tail that is held parallel to the dog's back usually suggests that the dog is feeling relaxed, whereas if the tail is held stiffly vertical, this usually means that the dog may be feeling aggressive or dominant.

A tail held much lower can mean that the dog is feeling stressed, afraid, submissive or unwell and if the tail is tucked underneath the dog's body, this is most often a sign that the dog is feeling stressed, fearful or threatened by another dog or person.

Chapter Six: Training and Behavior Modification

Paying attention to your dog's tail can help you to know when you need to step in and make some space between your dog and another, more dominant dog.

Of course, different breeds naturally carry their tails at different heights, so you will need to take this into consideration when studying your dog's tail so that you get used to their particular signals.

As well, the speed the tail is moving at will also give you an idea of the mental state of the dog because the speed of the wag usually indicates how excited a dog may be.

For instance, a slow, slightly swinging wag can often mean that the dog is tentative about greeting another dog, and this is more of a questioning type of wag, whereas a fast-moving tail held high can mean that a dog is about to challenge or threaten another less dominant dog.

Interestingly, two veterinarians at the University of Bari and a neuroscientist at the University of Trieste, in Italy, published a paper in which their research outlined that dogs' tails wagged more to their right side when they had positive feelings about a person or situation, and more to the left side when they were feeling negative.

While certainly a dog's tail can help us humans to understand how our dogs might be feeling, there are many other factors to take into consideration when determining a dog's state of mind.

What Does the Bark Mean?

Of course, our dogs bark for a wide variety of reasons, and every dog is different, depending upon their natural breed tendencies and how they were raised, and this section discusses some of the more common reasons why a Greyhound dog might be barking.

a) Communication: since the very first dog, they have communicated over long distances by howling to one another and when in closer proximity, barking to warn off other dogs approaching what they consider to be their territory or in excitement or happiness when greeting another member of the dog pack.

Now, our domesticated dogs have learned that barking for a wide variety of reasons, in a guard dog capacity to alert us to someone approaching the home, in anticipation of their favorite food, when they are afraid or frustrated, or to let us know they want to play is an effective way to get the

Chapter Six: Training and Behavior Modification

attention of us humans because barking is a difficult noise to ignore.

b) Danger: of course, our canine companions will bark to alert us to what they believe might be a dangerous situation, but how do we learn to understand the difference between what our dogs perceive as danger and what is truly dangerous, or indeed teach our best friends the difference?

We want our dogs to tell us when there is real imminent danger and, in this case, should the danger involve an unwanted intruder, we want them to bark loudly to possibly scare this threat away.

Unfortunately, many dogs are not quite as discerning as we humans might prefer, and as such they may end up barking during situations that we would consider inappropriate or just plain annoying.

When our dogs are barking for a reason we are not yet aware of, we need to calmly assess the situation rather than immediately becoming annoyed. We also need to remember that our dog's sense of smell, hearing and sometimes eyesight is far more acute than our own, so we need to give them an opportunity to tell us they just heard, saw or sensed something that they are worried or uncertain about.

Chapter Six: Training and Behavior Modification

Rather than ignoring our dogs (or yelling at them) when they are attempting to "tell" us that something is bothering them, even if we ourselves understand that the noise the dog just heard is only the neighbor pulling into their driveway, we need to calmly acknowledge the dog's concern by saying, "OK, good boy" or "OK, good girl" and then asking them to come to you. This way you have quietly and calmly let your dog know that the situation is nothing to be concerned about and you have asked them to move away from the target they are concerned about, which will usually stop the barking.

c) Attention: many dogs will learn to bark to get their owner's attention, just because they are bored or want to be taken outside for an interesting walk or a trip to the local park to chase a ball.

Our canine companions are very good at manipulating us in this way, and if we fall for it, we are setting up an annoying precedent that could plague us for the remainder of our relationship.

When a Greyhound is barking to gain their guardian's attention, even if it is warranted because (in this example) it is certainly time to go out for a walk, we must not be immediately manipulated. Instead, we need to calmly ask our

Chapter Six: Training and Behavior Modification

dog to do something for us, before leaping up and getting the leash to take our dog out.

After our dog has performed a calm and quiet task for us, such as sit and lie down, then we can decide to take our dog out for a walk.

In another example, often you will see a dog and their guardian at the local dog park playing fetch and when the human is not throwing that ball quickly enough to satisfy the dog's desire to run and fetch, the dog will be madly barking at the guardian.

Do not make the mistake of allowing your dog to manipulate you in this situation, because if you do, you will have created another bad habit that will very quickly become not just annoying to you, but also annoying to everyone else at the park.

Before throwing a ball or Frisbee for a dog that loves to retrieve, it is important to always ask the dog to sit and make eye contact with you.

Often the types of canines that are overly exuberant with chasing a ball or Frisbee have learned this barking behavior from their humans who allowed themselves to be literally at the beck and call of the dog, and they did this by throwing the ball every time the dog barked.

Chapter Six: Training and Behavior Modification

If you allow your dog to dictate to you when you will throw the ball, they will quickly learn that barking gets them their desired result, and you have just created an annoying, rude dog who is yelling at you in doggy language to do their bidding.

In this type of ball retrieving scenario, the dog has become ball "obsessed" and is no longer really paying attention to the guardian's commands, as they are solely focusing on where the ball is.

There are many situations in which a dog may bark to convey a certain message, such as letting you know when they need to go outside for potty, and of course, this is a good thing.

However, in all other situations where a dog is barking to demand attention or an object or food, this is when you need to ask them to do something for you, and then only if you want to give them what they are asking for, do you follow through.

Also, remember to stay calm when a dog is demanding attention because even negative attention can be rewarding for a dog that can then learn further habits that will not be particularly acceptable for the human side of the relationship.

Chapter Six: Training and Behavior Modification

d) Boredom or Separation Anxiety: many dogs, especially those who have not been properly trained or that have not been allowed to understand that they have rules and boundaries, and are treated like children, will bark loudly when left at home alone and they are bored or are feeling the anxiety of being alone.

Many times we humans believe that a dog is barking when being left alone because the dog is experiencing "separation anxiety", when in fact what the dog is really experiencing is the frustration of observing a member of the pack which they believe to be their follower (i.e. You) leaving them.

These dogs are loudly verbalizing this frustration and displeasure because, in the dog world, the pack follower does NOT leave the pack leader. In these cases, the humans really need the expert advice of a dog whisperer or dog psychologist to help turn the situation around and put the human guardian back in the driver's seat. Breaking a dog of the habit of loud barking when they are left alone can be solved in two different ways.

The most obvious being that you simply take your dog with you wherever you go, because after all, they are pack animals, and in order for them to be really happy and well balanced, they need the constant direction of their leader (which is supposed to be you).

Chapter Six: Training and Behavior Modification

The other, much lengthier and often more time-consuming way to solve a barking problem, involves hiring a professional to help assess why the problem has occurred and devise a plan that will work for your unique situation.

e) Fear or Pain: another reason our canine companions will bark is when they are very frightened or in pain and this is usually a type of bark that sounds quite different from all the others, often being a combination of a bark and a whine, or a yelping type of noise.

This is a bark that you will want to pay close attention to so that you can quickly respond and offer the dog assistance that they may need.

Whatever reason your dog may be barking, always remember that this is how they communicate and "tell" us that they want something or are concerned, afraid, nervous or unhappy about something, and as their guardians, we humans need to pay attention.

Managing Behavioral Problems In Your Dog

Despite their owners' training efforts, some dogs suddenly start exhibiting bad behaviors – even those that are

Chapter Six: Training and Behavior Modification

known to be on their best behavior most of the time. Many dog parents usually find it difficult to realize or acknowledge that their erstwhile loving and well-behaved dogs now have major behavioral issues. Sometimes, they fail to recognize because of the stigma associated with having a badly behaved pooch. The popular misconception among dog owners and enthusiasts is that dogs misbehave to show who is the boss or to show spite. Neither of these is true. Dogs do not have a sense of morality; they don't know what is wrong or right.

They just do the things that they do. So, it is impossible for your dog to intentionally try to hurt or spite you by exhibiting naughty behaviors. In most cases, a dog's behavioral problem is either fear or anxiety-related. As a dog parent, you must learn to understand your dog's way of conveying his feelings and thoughts via body language and signaling. If you get to read your dog accurately, then you can prevent possible behavioral issues and learn to manage existing ones better.

Some dogs also exhibit bad behaviors due to boredom. When your dog has nothing to keep him occupied, he might resort to chewing or digging. In a case like this, no other person than you should be held responsible. You are the one responsible for keeping your dog exercised and entertained. Only a lack of those two will make a dog turn towards bad behaviors to keep boredom at bay. In addition to ensuring

Chapter Six: Training and Behavior Modification

you maintain your dog's activity level and exercise him daily, you can equip yourself with knowledge on why and when a dog may become prone to a particular behavioral problem and then devise active ways of helping him overthrow the behavior.

Once you find that your Greyhound has behavioral issues, it can change your life in so many ways. You can either be the owner who adapts his or her lifestyle to meet your dog's needs and help him overcome his issue. Or, you can be the owner who continually exposes your dog to stressful situations to "correct" his problem. As the latter, you will only compound your dog's problem – especially if you are continually trying to get him to socialize as if that would make his behavior stop. Understandably, you might feel embarrassed when your dog acts up. But you don't have to feel shame or make your dog feel the shame. The first and best thing you should do is take appropriate steps to help your pet manage his behaviors problem. If the problem seems more than you can handle, you can then take your dog to a licensed animal behaviorist, veterinary, or certified dog trainer for professional help. You may need to evaluate your dog's mental and physical health to get to the root of his problem.

One by one, let's look at common behavioral issues in dogs and how you can manage or control them effectively.

Chapter Six: Training and Behavior Modification

Aggression

Aggression can be passive or active. Most times, it is exhibited subtly, making it hard for you to pick up fast. Whether passive or active, aggression is very dangerous behavior in dogs. When not managed effectively, it leads to euthanasia for most aggressive dogs. If your dog glares and bares his teeth at you or any other person when you attempt to get him off the furniture, that is a telltale sign of aggression. If he stands guard over his food bowl protectively, it's a sign.

If you prefer not to walk him because you know he won't be kind to dogs or animals he meets on the way, it is another sign. All these show that your dog has aggressive tendencies, which might lead to an actual accident someday.

If you notice aggressive signs or tendencies in your Greyhound dog, make your move immediately. Start setting limits with him, and only reward positive behavior at any time. Do not respond emotionally when he does something aggressive. Also, watch his diet. Sometimes, setting limits can make your pup's lousy behavior escalate. It might seem like you have no way around it. At this point, call a professional that can help to prevent serious harm in or outside your household. You can find someone in your local area or get them to refer you to an expert if they can't help.

Chapter Six: Training and Behavior Modification

Barking and Whining

The first thing to always keep in mind is that barking is natural for dogs, and some even find it enjoyable. Because it is part of who he is, it might be challenging to detect when barking becomes a behavioral problem in your pet. When you become aggravated or frustrated with constant barking or whining from your dog, try not to react in anger. Do not yell or pleat with him. If you bark back at him, he might take it as approval for him to continue his barking spree. Or, he sees it as a cue for him to repeatedly bark until you stop. To manage barking or whining in your Greyhound dog, train him to bark on command and teach him to be quiet on command too. So, whenever he starts barking, just use the quiet command to get him to hush.

Chewing

Like barking, it is natural for dogs to chew. All dogs chew because they need to. Once you accept this simple fact of life, you can take it upon yourself to purchase safe, acceptable, chew toys for your Greyhound dog. Instead of working his teeth on your household items, he can practice chewing on the toys. If he is bent on chewing objects around the house, do not let him loose. Crate or confine him to an area with his chew toys. Buy an array of chews until you find his favorite.

Chapter Six: Training and Behavior Modification

Digging

If your Greyhound dog loves to dig – again, I need to mention that digging is natural for canines, and you can't get your dog to stop. So, instead of fighting him, join him the next time he starts digging. Find a soft spot in your yard on the walk where he is likely to do less damage if he digs. Encourage him to dig in the spot. Get him to bury something that he can dig out back there. Praise him when he buries and digs back out. You can also set up a tiny sandbox for digging in the yard. If he takes his digging skills to an unacceptable part of the yard, it will be because you are not monitoring him or supervising him to an acceptable spot. This is also true for when he digs indoor. If your dog scratches out the floor, it is a sign that he is anxious or bored. Put him in a comfy and safe space, and let him play with his toys and chews. Or lead him outside to take a walk and guide him to his designated digging spot.

Jumping

If he is sitting, lying down, or confined, your pup can't jump up at anybody. Get a friend, neighbor, or family member to help you retrain this habit. Use the sit or stay command to restrain him to a spot when you have a visitor.

Chapter Six: Training and Behavior Modification

Practice the command with the help of someone else. Get the person to ring the doorbell, approach the door with your pet, and then ask him to sit right before you open. Wait until he complies. When the 'visitor' enters, give them some treats, and have them command your canine to sit. If he complies, they give him the treat. If he doesn't, they turn away from him for some moments. Repeat until he starts to adhere to no hesitation.

Dealing with Separation Anxiety

First thing's first: Know exactly what separation anxiety is, specifically for dogs. There's a fine line between this and other problems that you may encounter with dogs, and it's easy to confuse one with another. This can make treating the problem more complicated.

Separation anxiety is generally a behavioral problem. In other words, it's when your dog starts acting up in a way which is directly related to the fact that you're leaving. They're basically trying to express their distress of being left alone.

Chapter Six: Training and Behavior Modification

What Causes Dog Separation Anxiety?

As to why dogs react this way, nobody really knows. It happens to some dogs but not others. The disorder has been associated with changes in a puppy's circumstances, which usually has something to do with its "pack" or the group of dogs/people it has been accustomed to being around. Some of these include:

- Change of owner. The fact that the dog experiences a change in guardian makes it feel like it's been abandoned once. This can cause the fear of being left alone again.
- Drastic Changes in Schedule. When a dog is accustomed to being left alone for certain periods of time, the anxiety might trigger when it suddenly gets left alone for longer or different periods of time.
- Change in residence. Being left alone in an unfamiliar place is a lot different from being left alone in a place where a dog is used to hanging out while you're gone. This could cause some anxiety as well.
- Change of people around the dog. Yes, even dogs can be distraught over deaths in the family. The prolonged absence will definitely trigger the

anxiety as well. New members, whom the dog is unfamiliar with, can also have the same effect.

- How you leave the house. Yes, even your actions can directly cause or trigger the anxiety. You just don't know it, but making a big deal out of leaving the house (i.e., petting the dog a bit too much, or announcing that you're leaving) can provoke the feeling of being abandoned. It's quite logical for dogs to feel like something's up when all your actions scream, "Hey, I'm leaving you now!"

Typical Dog Separation Anxiety

For example, your dog could start acting more restless as you get ready to go out for work or school. The restlessness could come in many forms, such as when the dog actively follows you around the house, even when you're just going from room to room. Other weird things you'll notice are drooling, or a sudden disinterest in the things that usually entertain your dog (i.e., his favorite toy or food).

You will also notice this when you get home. Your dog will suddenly start acting up, or seem happier than you thought it would be to see you again. It will almost seem as if it were being rescued. And the weirdest part about it is that you will notice this even when you haven't been gone very lo

In some cases, you may also notice scratches on furniture or the sides of the doors that weren't there when you

Chapter Six: Training and Behavior Modification

left. And if you know that you've trained your dog to do his business outside or in a designated place, you'll also notice that he's been pooping in random places, like the kitchen floor or, worse, the carpet. You'll also notice scratches around entrances, as if the dog was trying to escape.

To sum up, these are things to watch out for:

- Signs of stress whenever you're about to leave
- No sign of eating whenever you're not around
- Urinating or defecating in improper places despite training
- Howling noises when you're not around
- Attempts to escape (i.e. gnawing or scratch marks on doors, window sills, cages, leashes, etc.)
- Injuries, resulting from uncontrolled behavior. Does your dog have broken nails or scratches from escape attempts or excessive scratching? Note: Be extra mindful of this one because this means that the anxiety has already reached a severe level.

Note: There are also some symptoms that aren't very easy to spot because dogs won't do these when their owners are around, such as pacing around in circles (like a person would if he or she were suffering from anxiety). One way to check is to peek through your window from outside your house, where you can see your dog. But dogs can be very sensitive and they'll be able to tell if you're around with their acute

Chapter Six: Training and Behavior Modification

sense of hearing and smell. So another way is to set up surveillance around the house to check what your dog is up to while you're gone.

Separation anxiety also varies in terms of severity:

- Some dogs fear being alone for even the slightest period of time, such that they follow you wherever you go around the house.
- Other dogs will just literally go to where you are in the house just to reassure themselves that you are still there (this one's particularly strange but it has been observed). When they're satisfied, they go back to whatever it was they were doing.
- Some dogs will not act up until you leave the house. This is when separation anxiety starts to become noticeable.
- Some dogs will only start to feel the anxiety when they've been left alone for a certain period of time.

Of course, the severity shouldn't be some gauge to make you think that it's still okay. If untreated, it'll eventually get worse, no matter how mild the anxiety was in the beginning.

But before you go out and find ways to treat this anxiety, you need to make sure that you're not confusing this with any other problem your dog could possibly be experiencing.

Chapter Six: Training and Behavior Modification

Distinguishing Separation Anxiety from Other Problems

Equally important to understanding dog separation anxiety is being able to distinguish it from other behavioral problems. Some of these problems are more severe while others are milder, when compared to separation anxiety. Either way, ruling out these other concerns will help you find the best treatment for your dog's problems.

1. Boredom or loneliness. For one thing, it could just be a case of boredom or loneliness. This can happen when you only have one dog, which is the case for most homeowners. While this doesn't mean you should get another dog (because they could both suffer from anxiety when you leave), you need to ascertain whether it's just a case of your dog not being able to find something fun to do.

Knowing the difference between this and separation anxiety is as easy as spotting a pattern. Sometimes your dog can get bored even when you're around. So if it only misbehaves when you're about to leave, it's definitely not just a case of boredom.

Also, you'll notice that dogs who are just bored will just mess around in less destructive ways. They'll chew on toys rather than furniture, and they don't usually howl or make noises.

2. Other things that could cause excessive urination. When your dog pees in the wrong place, it doesn't automatically mean he's suffering from separation anxiety. There could be other causes. For instance, your dog's hyperactive behavior could be a result of overexcitement. Yes, sometimes dogs get so excited that they end up peeing themselves.

It could also be because of fear or submission. Dogs often urinate to show that they are no threat. This is usually coupled with submissive postures and other things, so it's easy to distinguish them from separation anxiety.

But in either case, it will usually take place when you or someone else is around.

Dogs will also mark their territory with urine. This is different from excessive urination due to separation anxiety because they are controlled and are aimed at specific places.

3. Hyperactivity among young dogs. When dogs are young, they tend to be playful. So it's normal for them to do things that might not sit well with you, such as spilling their food, pooping in the wrong place, or ruining furniture. When you're checking your dog for separation anxiety, make sure you rule out the possibility that it's just a matter of puppies being a little too out of line.

Chapter Six: Training and Behavior Modification

Besides, separation anxiety has also been known to affect older dogs, or at least those that have been around long enough to become attached to you, the owner.

4. Lack of training. Remember, dogs will want to do whatever they want unless you teach them to behave. If they're misbehaving because you haven't had the time to teach them where to do what, don't immediately throw it off as dog separation anxiety.

5. Barking and Howling for a Reason. Dogs don't just make unnecessary howling or barking sounds because they don't want you to leave them. There are many triggers that would cause them to react aggressively. They could be afraid of an unfamiliar sound or something they don't usually see around the house. Pay attention to what they're trying to say to you.

6. Medical Related Causes. Excessive urination or defecation could also be caused by some kind of illness like diarrhea, so you will want to check with the vet just to make sure your dog is healthy.

Also check what kind of medication you're giving your dog. Some pet medications have all sorts of side effects, not only physiological but also behavioral as well.

You should also be aware of the difference between actual separation anxiety and its simulated form. The latter

Chapter Six: Training and Behavior Modification

happens when a dog realizes, through previous experience and some affirmation from the owner, that it can get attention by doing certain things, as bad as they may be. It's somewhat similar to what some children do when they misbehave to get the attention of their parents. Dogs will do this even when they know the result is going to be some kind of punishment—what's important is that they were noticed, which is what they crave.

The simulated kind of anxiety (which is hardly anxiety at all) must be dealt with by establishing leadership and training, which is another endeavor altogether. Thus, this confusion will only take place if you're uncertain whether your dog knows who the leader of the household is (ideally, it should be you).

Helping Your Greyhound Cope While You're Away

Separation anxiety is largely a behavioral problem, so you're going to need some time before you can condition your Greyhound dog not to be afraid of being left alone for long periods of time. There are some measures that you can take in order to help you cope with the issue.

Give your Greyhound **lots of things to play with.** The likeliness of anxiety increases when your dog only knows one thing to look forward to—and that's you. Giving your dog its

Chapter Six: Training and Behavior Modification

own favorite thing to play with or activity to do will provide an alternative to when you're not around to play or be with him. This includes getting lots of toys, or a space to play around in the house (preferably a place you don't usually hang out in). Using a variety of toys has been found to work to keep a dog busy throughout the day. You can also try leaving lots of treats in your dog's bowl for when you're not around.

Alternatively, those who are on a budget will find that even cardboard boxes can take so much of your dog's play time. Other simple things like ropes will work too. Just make sure you don't give your dog anything it can choke on

Take your Greyhound **with you, when possible.** This might sound counterintuitive to the whole idea of teaching a dog to be independent, but it might just be your only solution at times. Besides, if you like having your dog around with you and you can, why not? It's nice to have company when you're driving alone. Plus, this could be a great opportunity for you to train your dog to behave when following you around.

Leave your Greyhound **with a friend.** Obviously, it has to be someone that your dog recognizes and likes. Maybe some of your neighbors could help watch over your dog, keeping them company while you're gone. This is also a practical solution for when you'll be gone for a really long time.

Chapter Six: Training and Behavior Modification

This is also a good way to make sure your dog gets to know different kinds of people. Some have tried volunteering their dog to visit homes for the elderly or charity homes on a regular basis, and they usually bring joy and comfort to lots of people while forgetting about the problems of being alone.

Ever heard of daycare for dogs? Some communities have that, so consider yourself lucky if you're living near one. These centers can vary from place to place, but they all intend to be a place where you can leave your dog to be cared for while you're gone.

There are facilities that also offer to teach and train dogs, so you might also want this for your dog as well, especially when you've got no time to train him. This isn't to say that this is a perfect substitute to you training your dog, but it should at least keep your dog busy.

Get another dog, or pet. This is similar to the concept of getting toys, but another dog would mean a more permanent companionship. The loneliness wouldn't happen at all if your dog has a friend to play with.

Of course, you shouldn't just get another dog and just leave it with yours. You need to make sure that they get along with one another—even when you're not around. You can also try enlisting the help of a neighbor's dog. This doesn't

Chapter Six: Training and Behavior Modification

work for everyone, though. So give it a try for a few days and see how it goes.

Note: Just make sure you exercise this solution responsibly. Only take another dog into your home if you really want and can afford to sustain another one. Don't just get another dog to be the nanny or plaything of the one you already have.

Anti-Anxiety medication. This one's a bit tricky. In the same way that some people harbor the stigma against using medication to treat human behavioral problems, some owners advise against the use of medication to relieve their dog from anxiety.

But medication can be extremely helpful in some cases. For one thing, it's a great complement to any long term solution you might be using to deal with separation anxiety. Medication can also be helpful in more extreme cases of anxiety, such as when the dog gets a bit too violent for you to handle.

Of course, like most medication, it has to be administered under the advice of a veterinarian. Besides, you'll need a prescription for most cases. So only consider this when your dog's vet advises it.

Apply calming agents or aromatherapy. These are products, aside from usual medication, that can be used to

Chapter Six: Training and Behavior Modification

induce relaxation. The first thing that comes to mind would be pheromone diffusers. They're basically sprays that are left at home to diffuse stuff that will help your dog relax. They reduce stress, though they don't entirely eliminate anxiety.

There are also certain kinds of dog food that help induce relaxation. Some of them are in the form of chews or tablets so they're easier for a dog to eat. These also come in more organic forms, such as those made out of Chinese herbs. They're pretty much like products people use to relieve stress, only for dogs.

There are also "calming collars," which can be worn by your dog to release relaxing scents. Alternatively, there are special body wraps that are designed to induce relaxation by applying a comforting kind of pressure around your dog's body.

Try music. An empty house that's dead silent can cause even more anxiety. Having relaxing music play near your dog can help it relax. Most types of music that can relax people, such as classical music or music that simulates quiet, environment sounds, will work. But there are also sounds that are designed specifically to help dogs relax.

Leave a used shirt. Your dog will recognize the scent on your shirt and will feel better. It's like a very personalized

Chapter Six: Training and Behavior Modification

kind of aromatherapy—the kind that will make your dog feel less alone even when you're not around.

Employing any of these techniques will help you deal with your dog's separation anxiety. But one thing you'll notice is that none of them will be able to deal with your dog being left alone all the time. As mentioned before, these are just quick solutions to the problem until you can get around to dealing with the problem for the long term.

Going To The Park

Once you are ready to move to the park where you will encounter even more distractions, you will want to begin with using high value (or higher value) treats than you have been using indoors and in the enclosed area.

It is going to be harder for him to return, and therefore you want the reward to be extra special. You will also vary these treats so he doesn't know what to expect but he knows a really tasty treat is coming.

You might also want to vary the timing of the treat so he knows it's coming and it will be tasty but it might be in 1, 2, or 5 seconds (you will want to start varying the immediacy

Chapter Six: Training and Behavior Modification

of the reward when you are doing the outdoor enclosed training).

Try not to only call your Greyhound dog to you at the end of his walk. If you do it throughout the walk and reward him each time he comes back, he won't associate recall with the end of playtime.

At the end of the walk, make coming back fun and rewarding rather than something he doesn't like. I tend to play more at the end of the walk as I return to the entry gate of the park.

During the walk, you can vary his treat reward depending on how well he comes back to you when you give him his recall cue. If you call, and he continues to do what he is doing for a minute or two and then comes back, don't reward him right away.

Let him smell his treat and then let him start to move away from you. Call him again quickly (you want him to be set up to succeed, he needs to know what you want him to), and if he immediately turns around and comes back then reward and praise him. He will then be able to learn exactly what you mean, and what you want from him, when you give him his recall cue.

In the early stages, try rewarding him with one of his less favorite treats rather than no reward at all for taking his

Chapter Six: Training and Behavior Modification

time to come back. You want to ensure that he doesn't think he is being punished (by not getting his treat) for coming back, even if he took his time about it.

But remember, if you have already established a connection with your puppy and he finds you interesting, this will be much easier.

You can take your Greyhoundpuppy to the park on a long line but never let him off-leash until you are confident of his recall. You can let go of the long leash and if he runs too far you can stand on the end of it. It is much easier to do this than try and grab a shorter lead.

As you start to venture out on walks, your puppy won't be the only one meeting other similar animals to talk and play with.

It's important to pay attention to your puppy and to keep playing with him, and being fun, during a walk too. Standing around and talking to other dog walkers and ignoring him will mean, although he might be well exercised through all his running around, he is learning that you are not the most exciting thing in his life and his attention to you (and your recall cue) may not be 'heard'. He will simply tune it out as his attention is elsewhere.

Chapter Six: Training and Behavior Modification

Other Dogs And Their Communication Signals

The first thing that is going to happen when you can take your Greyhound out for real walks after his required vaccinations, is that he is going to meet other dogs the you both don't know.

Your puppy is going to be playful and excited to meet other dogs, but these dogs may not be so eager to have an excited puppy trying to play with them.

Older dogs (those over 2 years old) are not likely to want to play - in fact - dogs over 2 years old will tend to only play with dogs they know. Many will stop playing with other dogs altogether.

You will also need to pay attention to how the dogs you meet are reacting. Dogs will tell you far in advance if they are getting annoyed, are uncomfortable or feel threatened. I don't know how many times I have seen the owner of a dog watch as his dog tries to get another dog to play, and the dog being approached tries, again and again, to say 'no' until eventually, it runs out of options and snaps or even tries to bite to the dog who is pestering it.

These are the general stages to watch out for, and this will be the case both for your dog, and for the dogs that you meet. Try to pay attention to what dogs are telling each other and telling us.

Chapter Six: Training and Behavior Modification

If a Greyhound is displaying this behavior, then these are signs that he is feeling threatened, and is not happy with the attention of another dog, when it is close to him:

- Stage 1: Yawning, looking away, licking lips, moving away
- Stage 2: Panting, hackles up, and whale eyes (when a dog shows the whites of his eyes). This is a clear warning signal. If this still doesn't work then the next part will be a lip curl or snarl
- Stage 3: Lip curl or snarl or growl and possibly a snap. Then finally we will reach the stage we don't want to be
- Stage 4: A lunge towards the other dog (or the source of the 'threat') with barking as your dog tries to make the threat go away and then this may be followed by a bite.

How Dogs Greet Each Other

You need to be aware of other dogs, and, when you meet them, watch and understand what they are saying.

A dog running at another dog is not going to go down well. I am still surprised how often I see dog owners letting their dogs do this. If you see a dog running towards your puppy or dog, then there are a few things you can do.

Chapter Six: Training and Behavior Modification

As soon as I see this happening, and depending on how far away the other dog is, and how fast they are running, I will throw a ball or a stick to distract my dogs. This can sometimes encourage the other dog as well, and if I notice this, I just ignore the other dog and turn away with my dogs in the opposite direction. If my dog is playing further away from me, and he feels threatened by another dog, he comes back to me to be safe. If a dog runs towards him, he comes as close as he can - he sometimes tries to jump up into my arms.

My other dog tends to feel less threatened and seems to find it easier to deal with other dogs without resorting to aggression or fear. She must communicate well! She does this by a lip curl, then a growl, sometimes she adds in a whale eye, then an air snap but all of this is extremely unusual and she needs a lot of provocation. She always, like most dogs, starts with avoidance of the other dog if she can.

Others signs to watch out for include tails, are the tails up, and are the hackles up? Neither necessarily mean that the dog is aggressive but it indicates high adrenaline. If you notice this, distract your puppy or dog away from the other dog.

Two dogs that meet each other head-on and stare into each other's faces are not being friendly, but a dog that approaches from the side is being polite and asking for the intrusion into your dog's space.

Chapter Six: Training and Behavior Modification

A face greeting followed by a bottom sniff tends to be friendly. Bottom sniffing, generally, is fine and nothing to worry about.

If another dog puts his head across another dogs' shoulders this can be a sign of aggression and it can often be followed by mounting.

Just remember to always ask the other dog owner if it is ok for your puppy or dog to play with their dog. Do this especially if their dog is on a leash. Don't forget a dog that is on a leash might feel threatened by another dog, who is not on a leash, and who then tries to play with him. The dog on the leash will feel constrained, and this can lead to anxiety and a reaction to defend himself.

All of this is very important as your puppy begins his first walks. The experiences he has with other dogs at this stage are vital to how he views other dogs in the future, and if his experience is negative then he can easily build a negative association with other dogs - and be aggressive himself (he would see them as a threat).

One of the ways that you can help keep your puppy from getting over-excited around other dogs is to be more exciting yourself! Of course, you can also teach him sit-stay. Every time he sees another dog you will want to get him to sit and stay (and reward and praise him at each stage as he learns

Chapter Six: Training and Behavior Modification

this). You can use a clicker if you wish, and every time he learns a little bit more, click and reward.

As you first start to take your puppy out, he is likely to want to run up to other dogs himself. This is very different as it will be clear to most dogs that he is not being aggressive but curious and playful.

However, dogs older than 2 years old don't tend to like being harassed by a puppy so just make sure you don't create a situation that then leads your puppy to start fearing other dogs.

However, puppies learn by meeting other dogs and learning not to bother them, so try and teach them the basics with a dog you know.

How To Interact With Humans

You will already know some of these but a couple of points are worth re-stating. Don't let a stranger pat your Greyhound puppy or dog on the head. They can bring their hand slowly towards them from the side so he can sniff the hand.

If your Greyhound puppy starts to back away this is a sign of fear, and an early communication, so try to notice it and don't ignore it.

Chapter Six: Training and Behavior Modification

If your Greyhound starts to yawn, or lick his lips, then this is the next level of communication, and he is really trying to tell you and the other person that he is uncomfortable.

The final warning will be a bark. He will only get to this stage if nothing else has worked.

The best way to try and teach him that someone is not to be feared is to reward your puppy when he sees them to create a positive association. You can also try showing your puppy that there is nothing to fear by touching, perhaps shaking a hand, and quietly talking, and while you are doing this, reward with a high-value treat.

Games

Greyhounds love exercise and they need both physical and mental exercise.

When he is a puppy, you will only be walking him for around 20 minutes at a time and around 4 times per day. Don't be tempted to over-exercise him because this is not good for him (and try and prevent too many high impact games like jumping for a frisbee too often at this stage of his development).

You will use games for lots of reasons. One of the things you want to get your puppy to do is to watch you and know where you are. You always want to be moving around so that he knows he needs to keep an eye on you.

Chapter Six: Training and Behavior Modification

Hide and go seek is a great game to play. I love it more than the dogs and you probably will too.

This is game teaches them to pay attention to you. If you have forgotten how to play, hide behind a tree or a wall or any object. Let him run over to you and then come out, praise him and give him his treat.

A good way to play a game that reinforces paying attention to you (and can help remove any anxiety if other dogs are approaching) is to have them walk slightly in front of you and throw a really nice (and smelly) treat near you both for no apparent reason. This helps your puppy know that you might do something fun when he isn't expecting it.

A game I have found particularly good with my dogs is ball play. They play with their ball all the time and always need to come back to have me throw it for them. It means when I am out with them, they rarely leave me.

Dogs can alternate between balls, sticks and even pine cones (in the winter it might be a lost glove). They might surprise you with the things they love to retrieve (I call it 'fetch' and use this word as a cue). Frisbees are also very popular with Greyhound's.

Giving your Greyhound something to find will be a game he loves. You can do this in the home and teach him the game and what you want him to find. You can start with

Chapter Six: Training and Behavior Modification

cheese (find the cheese) and then introduce another item that you can hide outside (and old sock or t-short).

Finally, and one last example of a fun game is piggy in the middle. This is a great game for recall and everyone can join in.

As the name suggests, someone calls your puppy's name and gives them a treat or a toy, then someone else calls his name and he runs to them to get a treat or the toy, and so on. This is actually great fun and a great way to get comfortable when you go to the park for the first time.

Your Greyhound puppy will let you know what games and toys he likes best.

Chapter Six: Training and Behavior Modification

Chapter Seven: Vet Care for Your Greyhound

Choosing A Veterinarian

You may already know this but not all veterinarians are the same. They are only people after all. So, to find a good vet that you get on well with, may take some time and effort. Dog owners in most geographical areas tend to gravitate towards a particular vet. It is usually someone who is good

Chapter Seven: Vet Care for Your Greyhound

with dogs, trustworthy, great at the job and also has a good bedside manner with worried dog owners.

It is vitally important that you are completely happy with the vet that you choose for your Greyhound dog. This person may need to lead you through some very difficult times. So, a veterinarian who is hazy when sharing information or blunt towards you, may be very stressful for your entire family if you have an ill dog. A good way to find a popular vet in your local area is do some community research, ask other dog walkers, go onto Facebook and find community pages of dog owners in your local area. Find out from other people what their experiences are and learn from them.

As holistic care is growing in popularity, a number of holistic veterinary surgeons are becoming available. This is an option that I personally would urge you to consider; though it is usually more expensive, it is well worth it. The holistic vet has learned about veterinary science via the conventional route but has, in addition, put a lot of effort into learning natural health-care too. They will often treat symptoms with a mixture of less invasive therapies and conventional medicine, rather than simply use pharmaceutical options. In short, the holistic vet is more likely to look at the entire dog, diet, lifestyle and external influences on the health of your dog, as part of an overall holistic approach of care and treatment.

Why Vaccinate a Puppy?

Though you may not be able to prevent your Greyhound from developing certain inherited conditions if he already has a genetic predisposition, there are certain diseases you can prevent with vaccinations. During the first few weeks of life, your Greyhound puppy relies on the antibodies he receives from his mother's milk to fend off infection and illness. Once his own immune system develops, however, you will be able to administer vaccines to prevent certain diseases like canine distemper, parvovirus, and rabies.

Vaccinations for dogs can be divided into two categories: core vaccines, and non-core vaccines. Core vaccines are those that every dog should receive while noncore vaccines are administered based on your dog's level of risk. Depending on where you live and how often your Greyhound comes into contact with other dogs, you may not need to administer any non-core vaccines. According to the AVMA, recommended core vaccines for dogs include: distemper, canine adenovirus, canine parvovirus, and rabies. Non-core vaccines include: coronavirus, leptospirosis,

Chapter Seven: Vet Care for Your Greyhound

Bordetella bronchiseptica, canine parainfluenza, and Borrelia burgdorferi. You will need to speak to your veterinarian about non-core vaccines to determine which ones your Greyhound does and doesn't need. The rabies vaccine can be very stressful for dogs but, unfortunately, it is necessary in the United States due to the prevalence of rabies in wild animals. Rabies has been eradicated in the U.K. so dogs living in this area will not need rabies vaccines. Some veterinarians recommend that you only administer the rabies vaccine every three years. However, some states require an annual rabies vaccine, so be sure to check with your local council.

It is important to note however that a rabies vaccine should not be administered less than one month before or after a combination vaccine. The Greyhound that will be going into kennels may need to be immunized against canine kennel cough too. Most boarding establishments insist on it. Kennel cough immunization is via drops squirted up the dog's nose. It can be quite a stressful experience for dog and owner.

After the initial vaccination has been given, this is where the need for boosters becomes hazy. Some veterinarians state that a dog must get a booster every year whilst others think that it is a needless assault on the dog's immune system leaving the animal susceptible to illness. Although the yearly booster and associated parasite

Chapter Seven: Vet Care for Your Greyhound

prevention chemicals are standard procedure, at present more veterinarians are questioning the need for it. This is because each of the treatments has an effect on the dog's immune system and may leave the dog susceptible to passing viruses, illnesses which grow within the body, or bacteria in the environment.

Common Diseases and Viruses

a) Distemper: is a contagious and serious viral illness for which there is currently no known cure.

This deadly virus, which is spread either through the air or by direct or indirect contact with a dog that is already infected or other distemper carrying wildlife, including ferrets, raccoons, foxes, skunks and wolves, is a relative of the measles virus that affects humans.

Canine distemper is sometimes also called "hard pad disease" because some strains of the distemper virus actually cause the thickening of the pads on a dog's feet, which can also affect the end of a dog's nose. In dogs or animals with weak immune systems, death may result two to five weeks after the initial distemper infection.

Early symptoms of distemper include fever, loss of appetite, and mild eye inflammation that may only last a day or two. Symptoms become more serious and obvious as the disease progresses.

A puppy or dog that survives the distemper virus will usually continue to experience symptoms or signs of the disease throughout their remaining lifespan, including "hard pad disease" as well as "enamel hypoplasia", which is damage to the enamel of the puppy's teeth that are not yet formed or that have not yet pushed through the gums. Enamel hypoplasia is caused when the distemper virus kills the cells that manufacture tooth enamel.

b) Adenovirus: causes infectious canine hepatitis, which can range in severity from very mild to very serious, sometimes resulting in death.

Symptoms can include loss of appetite, coughing, increased thirst and urination, runny eyes and nose, vomiting, tiredness, bruising or bleeding under the skin, swelling of the head, neck and body, fluid accumulation in the abdomen area, jaundice (yellow tinge to the skin), a bluish clouding of the cornea of the eye (called "hepatitis blue eye") and seizures.

There is no specific treatment for infectious canine hepatitis and treatment is focused on managing symptoms while the virus runs its course. In severe cases, hospitalization and intravenous fluid therapy may be required.

c) Canine Parainfluenza Virus (CPIV): also referred to as "canine influenza virus", "greyhound disease" or "race flu", which is easily spread through the air or by coming into contact with respiratory secretions, was originally a virus that only affected horses.

This disease is believed to have adapted to become contagious to dogs, is easily spread from dog to dog, and may cause symptoms that become fatal.

While the more frequent occurrences of this respiratory infection are seen in areas where there are high dog populations, such as race tracks, boarding kennels and pet stores, this virus is highly contagious to any dog or puppy at any age.

A dry, hacking cough, difficulty breathing, tiredness, fever, sneezing, runny nose and eyes, depression, loss of appetite, and possible pneumonia are the symptoms. In cases where only a cough exists, tests will be required to determine whether the cause of the cough is the parainfluenza virus or the less serious "kennel cough".

Chapter Seven: Vet Care for Your Greyhound

While many dogs can naturally recover from this virus, they will remain contagious, and for this reason, in order to prevent the spread to other animals, aggressive treatment of the virus with antibiotics and antiviral drugs will be the general course of action.

In more severe cases, a cough suppressant may be prescribed, as well as intravenous fluids to help prevent secondary bacterial infection.

d) Canine Parvovirus (CPV): is a highly contagious viral illness affecting puppies and dogs. Parvovirus also affects other canine species including foxes, coyotes and wolves.

There are two forms of this virus (1) the more common intestinal form, and (2) the less common cardiac form, which can cause death in young puppies.

Symptoms of the intestinal form of parvovirus include vomiting, bloody diarrhea, weight loss, and lack of appetite, while the less common cardiac form attacks the heart muscle.

Early vaccination in young puppies has radically reduced the incidence of canine parvovirus infection, which is easily transmitted either by direct contact with an infected dog, or indirectly, by sniffing an infected dog's feces.

Chapter Seven: Vet Care for Your Greyhound

The virus can also be brought into a dog's environment on the bottom of human shoes that may have stepped on infected feces, and there is evidence that this hardy virus can live in ground soil for up to a year.

Recovery from parvovirus requires both aggressive and early treatment. With proper treatment, death rates are relatively low (between 5 and 20%), although chances of survival for puppies are much lower than for older dogs, and in all instances, there is no guarantee of survival.

Treatment of parvovirus requires hospitalization where intravenous fluids and nutrients are administered to help combat dehydration. Antibiotics will be given to counteract secondary bacterial infections, and as necessary, medications to control nausea and vomiting may also be given.

Without prompt and proper treatment, dogs that have severe parvovirus infections can die within 48 to 72 hours.

Other Diseases and Viruses

1) Rabies: is a viral disease transmitted by coming into contact with the saliva of an infected animal, usually through a bite. The virus travels to the brain along the nerves and once

Chapter Seven: Vet Care for Your Greyhound

symptoms develop, death is almost certainly inevitable, usually following a prolonged period of suffering.

If you plan to travel out of State or across country borders, you will need to make sure that your Greyhound has an up-to-date Rabies Vaccination Certificate (NASPHV form 51) indicating they have been inoculated against rabies.

Vaccinating dogs against rabies is also compulsory in most countries in mainland Europe, as is permanent identification and registration of dogs through the use of a Pet Passport.

Those living in a country that is rabies free (UK, Eire) are not required to vaccinate their dogs against rabies, unless they intend to travel.

2) Leishmaniasis: is caused by a parasite and is transmitted by a bite from a sand fly and there is no definitive answer for effectively combating Leishmaniasis, especially since one vaccine will not prevent the known multiple species.

In areas where the known cause is a sand fly, deltamethrin collars (containing a neurotoxic insecticide) worn by the dogs has been proven to be 86% effective. There are two types of Leishmaniasis: (1) a skin reaction causing

Chapter Seven: Vet Care for Your Greyhound

hair loss, lesions and ulcerative dermatitis, and (2) a more severe, abdominal organ reaction, which is also known as "black fever".

When the disease affects organs of the abdominal cavity the symptoms include loss of appetite, diarrhea, severe weight loss, exercise intolerance, vomiting, nosebleed, tarry feces, fever, pain in the joints, excessive thirst and urination and inflammation of the muscles.

Leishmaniasis spreads throughout the body to most organs, with kidney failure being the most common cause of death. Virtually all infected dogs develop this system wide disease and as much as 90% of those infected will also display skin reactions.

Affected dogs in the US are frequently found to have acquired this infection in another country.

Of note is that this disease is regularly found in the Middle East, the area around the Mediterranean basin, Portugal, Spain, Africa, South and Central America, southern Mexico and the US, with regular cases reported in Oklahoma and Ohio, where it is found in 20 to 40% of the dog population.

There have also been a few reported cases in Switzerland, northern France and the Netherlands.

Chapter Seven: Vet Care for Your Greyhound

NOTE: Leishmaniasis is a "zoonotic" infection, which is a contagious disease that can be spread between both animals and humans. This means that the organisms residing in the Leishmaniasis lesions can be communicated to humans.

Treatment in dogs is often difficult and the dog may suffer from relapses. Leishmaniasis poses a significant risk to the health of your dog, especially if you travel to the Mediterranean.

3) Lyme Disease: is one of the most common tick-borne diseases in the world, which is transmitted by Borrelia bacteria found in the deer or sheep tick. Lyme disease, also called "borreliosis", is also a zoonotic disease that can affect both humans and dogs and this disease can be fatal.

The Borrelia bacteria that causes Lyme's disease is transmitted by slow-feeding, hard-shelled deer or sheep ticks, and the tick usually has to be attached to the dog for a minimum of 18 hours before the infection is transmitted.

Symptoms of this disease in a young or adult dog include recurrent lameness from joint inflammation, loss of appetite, depression, stiff walk with arched back, sensitivity to touch, swollen lymph nodes, fever, kidney damage and rare heart or nervous system complications.

Chapter Seven: Vet Care for Your Greyhound

While Lyme disease has been reported in dogs throughout the United States and Europe, it is most prevalent in the upper Mid-Western states, the Atlantic seaboard, and the Pacific coastal states.

In order to properly diagnose and treat Lyme disease, blood tests will be required, and if the tests are positive, oral antibiotics will be prescribed to treat the conditions.

Prevention is the key to keeping this disease under control because dogs that have had Lyme disease before are still able to get the disease again. There is a vaccine for Lyme disease and dogs living in areas that have easy access to these ticks should be vaccinated yearly.

4) Rocky Mountain Spotted Fever (RMSF): is a tick-transmitted disease very often seen in dogs in the East, Midwest, and plains region of the US, and the organisms causing RMSF are transmitted by both the American dog tick and the RMSF tick, which must be attached to the dog for a minimum of five hours in order to transmit the disease.

Common symptoms of RMSF include fever, reduced appetite, depression, painful joints, lameness, vomiting and diarrhea.

Some dogs affected with RMSF may develop heart abnormalities, pneumonia, kidney failure, liver damage, or even neurological signs, such as seizures or unsteady, wobbly or stumbling gait. Diagnosis of this disease requires blood testing and if the results are positive, oral antibiotics will be given to the infected dog for approximately two weeks. Dogs that can clear the organism from their systems will recover and after being infected will remain immune to future infection.

5) Ehrlichiosis: a tick-borne disease transmitted by both the brown dog tick and the Lone Star Tick.

Ehrlichiosis has been reported in every state in the US, as well as worldwide. Common symptoms include depression, reduced appetite, fever, stiff and painful joints and bruising.

Signs of infection typically occur less than a month after a tick bite and last for approximately four weeks. There is no vaccine available.

Blood tests may be required to test for antibodies and treatment will require a course of antibiotics for up to four weeks in order to completely clear the organism from the infected dog's system.

Chapter Seven: Vet Care for Your Greyhound

After a dog has been previously infected, they may develop antibodies to the organism, but will not be immune to being re-infected.

Dogs living in areas of the country where the Ehrlichiosis tick disease are common or widespread may be prescribed low doses of antibiotics during tick season.

6) Anaplasmosis: deer ticks and Western blacklegged ticks are carriers of the bacteria that transmit canine Anaplasmosis. However, there is also another form of Anaplasmosis (caused by a different bacteria) that is carried by the brown dog tick.

Because the deer tick also carries other diseases, some animals may be at risk of developing more than one tick-borne disease at the same time. Signs of Anaplasmosis are similar to Ehrlichiosis and include painful joints, diarrhea, fever, and vomiting as well as possible nervous system disorders.

A dog will usually begin to show signs of Anaplasmosis within a couple of weeks after infection and diagnosis will require blood and urine testing, and sometimes other specialized laboratory tests.

Treatment is with oral antibiotics for up to 30 days, depending on how severe the infection may be. When this disease is quickly treated, most dogs will recover completely, however, subsequent immunity is not guaranteed, which means that a dog may be re-infected if exposed again.

7) Tick Paralysis: is caused when ticks attach themselves to a dog's skin and secrete a toxin that affects the dog's nervous system.

Affected dogs show signs of weakness and limpness approximately one week after being first bitten by ticks.

Symptoms usual begin with a change in pitch of the dog's usual bark, which will become softer, and weakness in the rear legs that eventually involves all four legs, which is then followed by the dog showing difficulty breathing and swallowing.

If the condition is not diagnosed and properly treated, death can occur. Treatment involves locating and removing the tick and then treating the infected dog with tick anti-serum.

8) Canine Coronavirus: while this highly contagious intestinal disease, which is spread through the feces of

Chapter Seven: Vet Care for Your Greyhound

contaminated dogs, was first discovered in Germany during 1971 when there was an outbreak in sentry dogs, it is now found worldwide. This virus can be destroyed by most commonly available disinfectants.

Symptoms include diarrhea, vomiting and weight loss or anorexia.

While deaths resulting from this disease are rare, and treatment generally requires only medication to relieve the diarrhea, dogs that are more severely affected may require intravenous fluids to combat dehydration.

There is a vaccine available, which is usually given to puppies because they are more susceptible at a young age. This vaccine is also given to show dogs that have a higher risk of exposure to the disease.

9) Leptospirosis: is a disease that occurs throughout the world that can affect many different kinds of animals, including dogs, and as it is also a zoonotic disease, it can affect humans, too.

There is potential for both dogs and humans to die from this disease.

The disease is always present in the environment, which makes it easy for any dog to pick up. This is because it is found in many common animals, such as rats, and wildlife, as well as domestic livestock.

Veterinarians generally see more cases of Leptospirosis in the late summer and fall, which is probably because that is when more pets and wildlife are out and about. More cases also occur after heavy rain falls. The disease is most common in mild or tropical climates around the World, and in the US or Canada it is more common in states or provinces that receive heavy rainfall.

The good news is that you can protect your dog from leptospirosis by vaccination, and while puppies are not routinely vaccinated against leptospirosis because chances of contracting the disease depend upon the lifestyle of the dog as well as the area in which the dog lives, it makes sense to vaccinate against this disease if you and your dog do live in an area considered a hot spot for leptospirosis, so ask your veterinarian.

City rat populations are a major carrier of leptospirosis.

Cold winter conditions lower the risk because the leptospira organisms do not tolerate the freezing and thawing of near-zero temperatures. They are killed rapidly by drying,

Chapter Seven: Vet Care for Your Greyhound

but they persist in standing water, dampness, mud and alkaline conditions.

Most of the infected domestic animals and wild animals that spread leptospirosis do not appear ill.

The leptospira take up residence in the kidneys of infected animals, which can include rats, mice, squirrels, skunks, and raccoons and when these animals void urine they contaminate their environment with living leptospira.

Dogs usually become infected after sniffing urine or by wading, swimming or drinking contaminated water that has infected urine in it, and this is how the disease passes from animal to animal. As well, the leptospira can also enter through a bite wound or if a dog eats infected material.

Additional Vaccinations

Depending upon where you and your Greyhound live, your veterinarian may suggest additional vaccinations to help combat diseases that may be more common in your area.

When Is a Puppy Vaccinated?

The first vaccination needle is normally given to a Greyhound puppy around six to eight weeks of age, which means that generally it will be the responsibility of the

Chapter Seven: Vet Care for Your Greyhound

breeder to ensure that the puppy's first shots have been received before their new owner takes them home.

Thereafter, it will be the new puppy's guardians that will be responsible for ensuring that the next two sets of shots, which are usually given three to four weeks after each other, are given by the new guardian's veterinarian at the proper intervals.

Do You Need a Pet Insurance?

Many new dog owners wonder whether pet insurance is a good option or whether it is a waste of money. The truth of the matter is that it is different in different cases. Pet insurance does for your pet what health insurance does for you; it helps to mitigate your out-of-pocket costs by providing coverage for certain services. While health insurance for humans covers all kinds of healthcare including preventive care, disease treatment, and accident coverage, pet insurance is a little more limited. Some pet insurance plans only cover accidents while others cover illnesses. Some plans cover certain preventive care options like spay/neuter surgery or vaccinations, but generally only during a puppy's first year.

The costs for pet insurance plans vary from one company to another and from one plan to another. Pet

Chapter Seven: Vet Care for Your Greyhound

insurance works in a very different way than health insurance when it comes to payment. With a health insurance plan, you might be asked to pay a co-payment to your doctor when you visit his office but the health plan will forward the remaining payment directly to the provider. With a pet insurance plan, you will be required to pay for the treatment upfront and then submit a claim to receive reimbursement for costs up to 90%. The actual amount a pet insurance plan will cover, varies from one plan to another and it may depend on the deductible amount you select as well.

Just as you would with a health insurance plan, having a pet insurance plan requires you to pay a monthly premium. As long as you remain current with those payments however, you are eligible to receive benefits from the plan. Keep in mind though, that most pet insurance plans have some kind of deductible in place. A deductible is a set amount that you must pay out-of-pocket before the plan will offer reimbursement for covered services. In many cases, pet insurance plans are useful only for large expenses like cancer treatments that you normally might not be able to cover at a moment's notice. It is not, however, generally cost-effective for things like annual vet exams and vaccinations.

De-Worming

Chapter Seven: Vet Care for Your Greyhound

De-worming kills internal parasites that your Greyhound dog or puppy may have. The two most common types of worms that may infest your canine companion are round worms and tapeworms, both of which can be passed on to humans.

NOTE: even though your living conditions may be completely sanitary, it is still possible for your dog to have internal parasites because this has nothing to do with where you live or how clean you keep your dog and your home. It is recommended by the Center for Disease Control (CDC) that puppies be dewormed every 2 weeks until they are 3 months old, and then every month after that, in order to control worms.

Puppies are usually regularly wormed by the breeder before the puppies are taken to their homes, however, many veterinarians recommend worming dogs for tapeworm and roundworms every 6-12 months.

The health risks to your Greyhound puppy or dog include diarrhea, vomiting, slow growth, and in serious cases a bowel blockage or pneumonia, even death.

Most puppies and dogs will experience worms at some stage in their life and thankfully the problem can be easily and swiftly eliminated with worming medication.

Chapter Seven: Vet Care for Your Greyhound

Healthy And Sick Dog

A healthy Greyhound dog is a cheerful animal with a shiny coat, clean and clear eyes, with a slightly damp and cold nose, however, it must be noted that the last sign is not always reliable. A healthy dog responds to the call of the owner, willingly fulfills commands. A healthy dog has a good appetite, bowels are emptied regularly, and urination is normal. The mucous membranes of the mouth, eyelids are clean, pale pink in color. Breathing is even.

A sick Greyhound differs markedly from a healthy individual. Any disease causes a number of more or less serious disorders in her body.

First, there are changes in your pet's behavior. The dog is depressed, lies a lot, tries to hide in a dark place, gets up reluctantly when called. With some pathologies, she does not want to go to bed, stands for a long time and is only completely exhausted, takes a forced lying or other posture (for example, with pain in the spine, with heart disease, with a fracture of a limb, when the dog is holding her in weight).

A sick pet is either indifferent to others, or vice versa, abnormally excited, too mobile, and can be aggressive even towards close people. Appetite is disturbed: the dog eats poorly or completely refuses to feed, or its appetite is increased, even perverted. Swallowing solid food is difficult, and choking may occur when swallowing even liquid and chopped food. Increased thirst or, conversely, hydrophobia may be observed. A cough may appear, indicating inflammation in the throat, larynx or trachea, lung and heart disease. A sudden, violent, persistent cough is caused by a foreign body entering the trachea.

Secondly, there are external signs of the Greyhound dog's disease. The coat turns from shiny and glossy to dull, tousled. Baldness of certain areas of the body, rash, scratching, non-healing wounds and eczema are possible. Bad breath may occur, which, for example, is often caused by eczema located in the folds of the lips, while in other dogs it is usually associated with heavy tartar deposits and ulcerative stomatitis. The areas of the affected skin with demodicosis smell unpleasant. The mucous membranes of the mouth and eyelids are pale, bluish or icteric. The activity of the gastrointestinal tract is disrupted: vomiting, diarrhea, constipation, accumulation of gases in the intestines appear, blood, foreign bodies, worms appear in the feces. Purulent discharge from the nose, eyes and other organs of the dog appears, as well as bad breath, ears and other cavities. Urination is impaired, the color of urine, and its amount change. There are deviations from the norm in body temperature, pulse, respiration.

Chapter Seven: Vet Care for Your Greyhound

The listed signs of a sick animal usually do not appear at the same time, one or several are pronounced.

With a severe degree of the disease or with the development of a particular disease, the number of pathological signs increases.

It is possible to speak about the recovery of an animal only after the disappearance of all painful manifestations inherent in one or another pathological process.

When Your Greyhound Eats Something They Shouldn't

Greyhound puppies explore the world with their mouths, which often results in biting, chewing, and potentially swallowing things that shouldn't be consumed. This section covers what to do if your puppy has eaten something that's not good for them and how to handle these situations if they arise.

Poisoning

If your Greyhound accidentally ingests a toxic substance, call your vet or poison control immediately. The Pet Poison Helpline (855-764-7661) is staffed with experts who can help you determine what you should be watching for and how you should proceed following an ingestion. Never try to induce vomiting in your puppy unless instructed to do so by a professional; vomiting up certain substances can cause serious issues. Signs and symptoms of poisoning will vary greatly depending on what your puppy has eaten.

Choking

Some items, if swallowed, can become lodged in your Greyhound's mouth or throat. This is a life-threatening situation, as a foreign object can obstruct the airway and prevent your puppy from breathing. Signs that your puppy might be choking include pawing at their mouth, gagging or gasping, not responding, or losing consciousness. If your puppy can't breathe, use both hands to open their mouth, one hand on the upper jaw and one on the lower. (Be cautious of the potential bite risk when doing this; panicked animals are not generally mindful of human fingers.) If you can see and easily hook the obstruction with your finger, you should do so, but if it's too deep and you must reach or dig for it, stop and transport your puppy to the vet immediately. Attempting to reach a deeply lodged obstruction can push it deeper and cause damage to the surrounding tissues.

Swallowing Foreign Objects

Swallowing foreign objects is a common concern with Greyhound puppies. Dogs don't readily know what's edible and what's not, and their standards of what may make a tasty snack differ greatly from ours. Foreign bodies can be a medical emergency if swallowed and should not be taken lightly. If a foreign object is tightly obstructed, it can quickly cause damage to the surrounding tissues, potentially resulting in death.

If your dog has just ingested a foreign item, call your vet to see if they recommend inducing vomiting. Depending on the size, texture, and material, some objects (such as baby socks) can be thrown up safely, whereas others can cause significant damage. Some smaller items might be able to pass through your dog's system with no issue. Signs that your puppy may have ingested a foreign item include vomiting, diarrhea or constipation, lack of appetite, lethargy, and depression. Your vet can take an X-ray of your dog's intestinal tract to search for the foreign item. Depending on its place in your dog's digestive system, the vet may recommend removing it surgically or endoscopically.

Stress

Chapter Seven: Vet Care for Your Greyhound

Short Term Stress

Stress is a biological response to an apparent threat. Biologically, the dog's body is programmed to keep the animal safe by reacting in a certain way to fear. The natural reaction, at a very basic level, involves the release of very specific hormones into the dog's body which prepare the animal to deal with a threatening situation.

The subconscious preparation that happens within the body of the dog involves sending adrenaline to each of the muscles thus preparing the dog for a fight or to take flight.

In addition to this, the dog's body redirects energy to the places that will best provide immediate safety. The heart rate raises whilst digestion, immunity and reproductive organs are literally 'switched off' as each of these are secondary functions to the need for basic survival.

The dog's decision at this point will usually depend on a mixture of genetic responses and his experience of life so far. Similarly, the things that a dog gets stressed about will be determined by the animal as an individual.

Some dogs, for instance, will get stressed in the car whilst others are stressed and fearful during fireworks season. Dogs that have not been properly socialized will often get stressed in the company of other dogs, simply because they don't know how to react.

Chapter Seven: Vet Care for Your Greyhound

Long Term Stress

So now we know, in very basic terms, what an immediate stress reaction does to the dog. Now, let's take a look at exactly what long term stress does to a dog.

Long term stress leads to dysfunction in digestion, loss of general condition and eventually many illnesses because the immune system is busy elsewhere.

What Causes Stress?

This is where it gets really interesting. Stress can be triggered by anything at all. This is a subject where dogs and humans are very much alike.

Common causes of stress are;

- Allergies
- Under socialization
- Lack of training
- Insufficient exercise
- An insecure environment
- Excessive noise
- Over exercise
- Agility and other sports that cause adrenaline release in the body of the dog.

Chapter Seven: Vet Care for Your Greyhound

Just as we are all different and some of us can deal with a lot of stress before we cave in, dogs are exactly the same. Some can deal with with anything at all and others cope with things by becoming stressed about them. Your job as the guardian and friend of a Greyhound, is to recognize any stressors in the life of your dog and make changes.

For instance, if your Greyhound eats food with known allergens then change his food type. If your Greyhound is worried about other dogs, do some careful socialization training. If your friend is completely stressed during firework season, take some precautions to help him through it, such as Bach Flower remedy, or simply comforting him and not leaving him alone.

Chapter Eight: Showing Your Greyhound

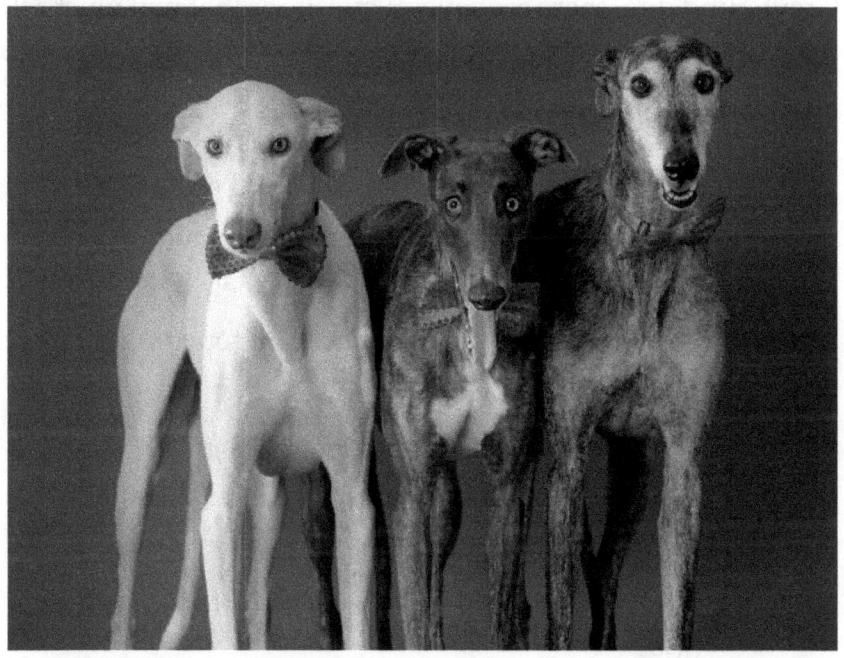

You may choose that you wish to show your Greyhound dog. If you choose that you wish to show your Greyhound dos, there are a couple of things to bear in mind.

To start with, showing dogs could be a great deal of work. You are going to want to be certain that you have the appropriate types and information so that you could get registered for the show sufficiently early. You are going to additionally want to be certain that you are prepared to show dogs, implying that you have had the appropriate amount of time to work with your Greyhound dog.

Chapter Eight: Showing Your Greyhound

When you are figuring out whether to show your Greyhound dog, there are several questions that you must ask yourself so that you understand you are showing the appropriate kinds of dog.

- Does your dog comply with breed requirements?
- Is your dog properly trained, or could you train him/her quickly to walk within the ring?
- Is your dog cozy with somebody touching him/her and raising her up?
- Is your dog cozy with other dogs?
- Is your dog going to bite, or will he/she attempt to trouble the other animals?
- Are you prepared to take a trip to shows with your dog?
- Is a dog showing anything you believe you would like as a pastime?

The responses to these questions are going to aid you to ensure that you have actually offered ample information about your dog and that you understand your dog will be great in the ring. This is a thing that you will wish to think thoroughly about prior to showing your dog.

Showing a dog could result in excellent things for your dog. He/she is going to have the ability to be much better trained, and as you undergo more shows, he/she is going to

Chapter Eight: Showing Your Greyhound

discover much more. Additionally, you are going to have the ability to manage your dog more.

Having accreditations or championships from being shown is an essential thing in the realm of breeding. Sometimes individuals are going to wish to have your pups if the parents have actually been shown since it reveals that your dogs are fantastic instances of the kind of dog which they are searching for.

Transporting Your Dog

The rules for transporting dogs are determined by the carrier. The most common rules apply to keeping a dog on a leash and putting on a muzzle. Remember that you know your Greyhound very well, but first of all you can't predict how your dog will behave in a new situation, in the crowd or when traveling next to another unknown dog. Secondly, carriers are obliged to ensure the safety of all passengers, hence the leash and muzzle. Four-legged dogs are most often forbidden to sit on seats, while owners are ordered to carry a health booklet with them with them, along with the vaccinations. Some regulations may not apply to assisting dogs, four-legged guides for the blind or police dogs. So how

Chapter Eight: Showing Your Greyhound

to travel with a four-legged person by different means of transport?

Check your dog's health

Make sure your Greyhound has a valid rabies vaccination entered in the health booklet, is dewormed, and his general state of health allows you to travel longer without any problems. If you're going abroad, don't forget to update your dog's passport and check the requirements for transporting animals into your country.

Remember to protect against ticks

Regardless of the destination of your journey, it is essential to protect your Greyhound from ticks! The higher the temperature and humidity of the environment, the more of them. There are many anti-tick products in various forms on the market. The most frequently used and most popular among owners are collars and spot-on's (so called drops). Drops are perfect when we go to the water.

Check the weather for your trip and don't be surprised!

Chapter Eight: Showing Your Greyhound

If it's supposed to be warm, prepare your pet for high temperatures. Recently, a cooling jacket for dogs has become very popular. Just soak it in water, squeeze it out and put it on. The jacket gives off excess heat as a result of evaporation of water. In addition, its bright color reflects sunlight, reducing heat.

Chapter Eight: Showing Your Greyhound

Chapter Nine: Breeding Your Greyhound

Breeding dogs is a thing that needs a great deal of effort, and something that needs a lifetime dedication on your part. For that reason, if you want to be a Greyhound dog breeder, you need to have some significant aspects of your life which focus on dogs.

Choosing When To Breed

When you are raising Greyhound dogs to breed them, you will want to determine when you need to start the

Chapter Nine: Breeding Your Greyhound

breeding procedure. This is really essential since you do not wish to breed a dog if they are too young, and you additionally do not wish to wait too much.

There are certain great guidelines to stick to when you are choosing when to breed your Greyhound dogs. To start with, remember that you need to be ready for your dogs not to breed as you would wish them to. Even if you have a female and a male does not indicate that they are going to breed properly, and it does not imply that they are going to produce the pups you are after.

A great guideline to follow is that you must never ever breed a female dog on her initial heat cycle, and not even on her 2nd if you can do something about it. You ought to wait till she is at least a year and a half old, or on her 2nd heat cycle, whichever precedes. A lot of breeders wait until the female is 2 years of age to begin breeding.

Male dogs are able to breed the moment they are a year old, at a minimum, although they may not develop completely before then, so you wish to watch on your male and ensure that he is the appropriate age.

Keep in mind in case you have a female and a male dog that are living together, you are going to want to keep them apart throughout the heat cycles that you do not want them to breed in. Your dogs are going to breed in case they get the

Chapter Nine: Breeding Your Greyhound

opportunity since dogs do not understand that they are too young, and they will not realize if they have actually already been bred on their final heat cycle. For that reason, it depends on you to make certain that breeding just happens when you want it to occur.

The initial thing to consider is age. Then, it is essential to think of how frequently. Responsible breeders are not going to breed their dogs on back-to-back heat cycles. So, in case your female dog has actually had a litter of pups on single cycle, even if she had no issues and the litter achieved success, you do not wish to breed her on the following one. Make certain that she is kept from the male dog up until you are prepared to breed her once again.

Breeding Process

When you have all the things established, you can start to really do the breeding procedure for your dogs.

Once again, ensure that the dogs you are breeding are the appropriate age. You wish to make certain that you have waited for the correct quantity of time, and that the dogs you are breeding will be at the top shape for breeding.

Chapter Nine: Breeding Your Greyhound

Take your dogs to the veterinarian and ensure that they are prepared to be bred. Have them looked at, and make certain that they are in the appropriate health to breed. Get them up to date regarding their shots to ensure that you understand you are going to be breeding dogs which are in good shape and are not going to have any shot issues to stress over.

Then, you could allow nature to work its magic. Your female dog is going to enter into the season around two times per year. This is going to be different depending upon the breed. You are going to know that she is heading into the season since there is going to be a discharge that is visible from her. Anywhere from 5 to 10 days after you see the discharge, the male dog is going to have an interest in her. The majority of the time, male dogs have an interest in the female well before she has an interest in them, so do not be dissuaded if it does not occur as quickly as you wish it to take place. Just enable your dogs to be alone together, and when the time is appropriate, they are going to take care of business.

The majority of breeders do not do any help when it pertains to the actual breeding. Nevertheless, with some tinier breeds, or with females that require support, some slight support, such as holding the female in place, is needed. You are going to want to experiment and see if your dogs require any help, or if they are prepared to breed immediately.

Chapter Nine: Breeding Your Greyhound

As soon as your dogs have actually bred, you are going to want to treat your female as if she is pregnant. For the initial four weeks, keep her on her routine diet plan, however, make certain that she has access to food any time she is starving. Do not get her too fired up and enable her to do what she wishes to do. Keep exercising her, nevertheless.

For the subsequent eight weeks, start giving puppy food to your pregnant dog. This is going to assist her in getting the appropriate nutrients. Do not do this prior to the fifth week, nevertheless, as her body has to produce a number of things at the beginning of her pregnancy to be healthy-- and as pup food may not enable this to take place.

Let your mom dog do what she wishes to do, and remember that she may be moody or more caring than common. Keep her with you and keep her working out too. This is really essential to the excellent growth of young puppies.

Birthing Process

When it comes time to deliver your pups, there are a couple of things that you must understand so that your pups can be healthy and pleased and that your mom dog is going to be safe.

Chapter Nine: Breeding Your Greyhound

Firstly, keep an eye on the due date. Your veterinarian can assist you with this and, therefore, can provide you with information concerning your particular type.

As the due date gets nearer and nearer, make certain that you are collecting your supplies. Your mom's dog must have a birth box that she is able to go to. Ensure that this remains in the area where you want your young puppies to be born. It ought to remain in an area that you frequently enter, such as your bedroom-- and if feasible, it ought to remain in the location where your mom dog sleeps during the night. This is going to enable her to be cozy with the pups.

As it gets nearer, assemble a birthing set for yourself.

- Tidy rags
- Gloves
- Scissors
- Iodine
- Infant mouth and nose cleaner
- q-tips
- Eyedropper
- A scale

Make certain that the mom is cozy in her birth box, and after that, wait.

When the time arrives, you are going to have the ability to tell. Your mom dog is going to spend additional time

Chapter Nine: Breeding Your Greyhound

nesting within the box. As she enters into labor, she is going to typically sit up and pant. You are going to manage to see the contractions that she is having within her body

Shift her to the birth box, and after that, wait with her. The majority of mom dogs do not like to have pups alone in case they have great relationships with their owners.

As the pups start to be born, you are going to need to choose whether you wish to help. The majority of the time, nature will take its course, and the mom is going to deliver the young ones.

In case the mom is laboring for more than an hour after you have observed the sac and the puppy has actually begun to be born, you are going to wish to call a veterinarian to assist you. The pup may be stuck. Alternatively, you could carefully guide the puppy out by pulling lightly but strongly with a wet and soft rag. Attempt not to break the sac open as the puppy is still within the mom dog. In case the sac does break, you are going to want to get the pup out immediately.

When the pup is out of the mom, she needs to burst the sac and lick the pup's face. In case she does not do this within seconds, you could burst the sac utilizing your scissors or fingernails.

Present the pup's face to the mom and get her to lick it tidy. You ought to hear the pup starting to breathe. In case the

Chapter Nine: Breeding Your Greyhound

mom does not lick the puppies face, you may want to clean it and clear the pup's throat and nose. You could perform this by utilizing the infant cleaner or the rag. The majority of the time, the mom is going to clear the passages so the child is able to breathe.

In between pups, the mom needs to tidy up the majority of the mess and needs to clean up the little one. Attempt not to get in her way except if she is having issues with something. You could place the pup onto a nipple while she accomplishes this. Healthy puppies should wish to suck immediately.

The majority of pups are going to be born within hours of one another. If the mom dog is laboring and it has actually been more than a handful of hours in between pups, you must call a veterinarian since something could be wrong.

As soon as all of the puppies have actually been born and the mom is laboring no more, you are able to weigh the puppies and change the bed linen in the box. The mom is going to wish to go outdoors to go to the restroom, most likely. When she returns, make certain that you place the pups onto the nipples to eat.

Your primary objective must be to help the mom if she requires it. Look at them every now and then. It is always an excellent idea to move pups nearer to the mom in case they

Chapter Nine: Breeding Your Greyhound

have actually been moved, and to place them on a nipple to ensure that they are able to eat.

There are certain things to keep an eye out for immediately when it concerns pups. You must look for veterinarian's assistance instantly if:

- A puppy does not eat
- A pup isn't walking around
- A puppy is being pressed sideways by the mom
- A puppy is loud.

Healthy puppies need to:

- Stay mainly peaceful
- Put on weight every day
- Be proactively eating
- Breathe at a regular rate
- Appear content.
-

Understanding Various Stages Of Growth

Each stage of life brings new milestones for puppies. Let's look at the various stages of growth, what's occurring during each one, and what you can expect to witness, both physically and socially, as your puppy matures.

0 to 2 weeks

Chapter Nine: Breeding Your Greyhound

Your puppy is considered a "neonate" (newborn) at this stage and is completely dependent on their mother for everything, including nutrition, hygiene, and elimination. Puppies will snuggle next to their mom and "heap" on top of one another to keep warm, as they can't regulate their body temperatures yet. Their eyes and ears are closed, so they're learning about their world entirely through touch and smell—but at this age, puppies can only move by crawling, so they're not doing much exploration. They spend most of the day nursing, sleeping, and growing.

Don't Take Your Puppy Home Too Soon!

The most important thing to know about your puppy's early development is that they shouldn't leave their mother before 8 weeks of age. Puppies require diligent, around-the-clock care during these critical weeks, and they learn a lot from their mothers and littermates. Early removal from the litter might result in a puppy who's less capable of adapting to new situations later in life. Studies show that puppies who are removed from their mothers before 8 weeks are more prone to attention-seeking behaviors, reactivity to noises, fearfulness on walks, excessive barking, aversion to strangers, and inappropriate play biting.

2 to 4 weeks

Chapter Nine: Breeding Your Greyhound

This is considered the transitional phase in a puppy's development. Their eyes and ears open, and their senses are rapidly developing. Their teeth start to emerge, although they won't become a full set of baby teeth until 6 to 8 weeks of age. Your puppy is becoming increasingly mobile, learning to walk at around 3 weeks of age. Walking is followed by scampering and other faster, albeit clumsy, movements. Puppies are also now learning to bark, wag their tails, and communicate with one another. Soon they'll be able to eliminate on their own without their mom's help.

4 to 8 weeks

During this time, puppies start to nurse less and less, until eventually they wean off mother's milk completely. That means they'll start eating solid foods like soft puppy food and eventually kibble. There is a steep increase in their motor skills and function in this period, as most of their waking hours are spent playing with littermates. Through this play, puppies develop and rehearse various social skills and learn "bite inhibition" (not applying too much pressure with their teeth). Although they're becoming more independent, it's important that puppies stay with their mom and littermates until they're 8 weeks of age at a minimum. Removing the puppy too soon can interfere with important social development.

8 to 16 weeks

Chapter Nine: Breeding Your Greyhound

This is when you're likely bringing your new puppy home. It's important to know that they're now in what we call the "socialization period," which plays a crucial role in shaping their future personality. The critical socialization period is between 3 and 12 weeks, but socialization deficits through 14 weeks of age can lead to behavioral issues later on. Your puppy is learning by association, so use treats and patience to make sure that all interactions and experiences they have during this time are positive and fun! Simultaneously, between 8 and 11 weeks of age, your puppy may experience their first fear period, where novel stimuli may alarm or spook them. During this stage, it's important to try to protect your puppy from frightening experiences, as they can leave a permanent mark. Don't pressure them to approach or interact with anything they're nervous about, and use rewards to make new experiences positive for them.

4 to 12 months

Your puppy's socialization period ends around 12 to 14 weeks of age—but that doesn't mean you can sit back and rest. Continuing to expose your dog to the world and new experiences, at the dog's pace and in a positive way, is important during their entire first year so that they can practice learned behaviors in new environments.

At around 6 months, your puppy is now considered an adolescent, whether they've become sexually mature or not.

Chapter Nine: Breeding Your Greyhound

This is a busy and active phase of life in which they continue to work on developing and maturing their social skills. Regular interactions and play with other dogs keep their social skills sharp and can also be a great outlet for their abundance of energy at this age. Regular obedience and manners training can help make these busy dogs manageable and more enjoyable to be around, while also tiring out their brains. Mental stimulation can prevent boredom and the behavior problems that go with it.

1 to 2 years

Around 18 months of age, your dog may start testing the boundaries of known cues or commands. I jokingly call this the "juvenile delinquent" phase of life. In other words, your dog is now a teenager! This may come with certain behavioral changes. You may notice a shift in your dog's overall sociability anytime between 1 and 3 years of age. They might be more selective about whom they play with, what kind of play they tolerate freely, or their desire to play in general. These are normal changes and will vary for each dog.

Chapter Nine: Breeding Your Greyhound

Conclusion

The Greyhound is perfect for young families who are always on the go and for those who want a loyal and loving companion.

Your Greyhound may have all the typical characteristics but it will also have its own personality, much like a human being. Like any individual, your Greyhound will have its own idiosyncrasies. Thus, when you get to know and start to train your Greyhound, make sure that you establish a caring and friendly environment. Continue to shower your Greyhound with praise and be firm with it when it misbehaves. Just like a child, your Greyhound needs to learn what is expected of him and to be taught the difference of right from wrong. But in return, your Greyhound will love you fully and unconditionally.

When possible, take your Greyhound with you when you leave the house. Take it out on car rides. Gradually lengthen your trips until your Greyhound is used to travelling. You may even take it on overseas trips whenever possible.

Being exposed to new places and people when you are with it will help your Greyhound increase its confidence in itself and in you as its master. Sharing many adventures will mean sharing happiness, excitement and a deep and abiding friendship between the two of you and among members of the family.

Care for your Greyhound as you would any loved one and you will be rewarded tenfold. You will soon find that

Conclusion

once you establish a good rapport and a trusting and solid relationship with your Greyhound, you and your Greyhound will both enjoy many wonderful years together of friendship, camaraderie and love.

Glossary of Terms

Adoption – A process in which a rescued pet is placed into a permanent home.

Acute Disease – refers to a disease or illness that manifests quickly

Agility – This is a sport in which the dog handler guides and instructs the dog through a course of obstacles while being timed. Accuracy through this obstacle course is paramount. The dogs must complete the obstacle course without a leash or toys (or food) as incentives. The handler can only use voice, movement and various body signals in order to direct the dog.

AKC – American Kennel Club, the largest purebred dog registry in the United States

Almond Eye – Referring to an elongated eye shape rather than a rounded shape

Apple Head – A round-shaped skull

Balance – A show term referring to all of the parts of the dog, both moving and standing, which produce a harmonious image

Beard – Long, thick hair on the dog's underjaw

Best in Show – An award given to the only undefeated dog left standing at the end of judging

Bitch – A female dog

Glossary of Terms

Bite – The position of the upper and lower teeth when the dog's jaws are closed; positions include level, undershot, scissors, or overshot

Blaze – A white stripe running down the center of the face between the eyes

Board – To house, feed, and care for a dog for a fee

Breed – A domestic race of dogs having a common gene pool and characterized appearance/function

Breed Standard – A published document describing the look, movement, and behavior of the perfect specimen of a particular breed

Buff – An off-white to gold coloring

Canine- a term for dog.

Canine Teeth- also known as eye teeth, the largest teeth found in the dog's mouth. They are long, curved teeth on either side of the mouth, top and bottom.

Chronic Disease – refers to a disease that will last indefinitely.

Clip – A method of trimming the coat in some breeds

Coat – The hair covering of a dog; some breeds have two coats, and outer coat and undercoat; also known as a double coat. Examples of breeds with double coats include Shiba Inu, German Shepherd, Siberian Husky, Akita, etc.

Condition – The health of the dog as shown by its skin, coat, behavior, and general appearance

Glossary of Terms

Crate – A container used to house and transport dogs; also called a cage or kennel

Crossbreed (Hybrid) – A dog having a sire and dam of two different breeds; cannot be registered with the AKC

Dam (bitch) – The female parent of a dog;

Dock – To shorten the tail of a dog by surgically removing the end part of the tail.

Double Coat – Having an outer weather-resistant coat and a soft, waterproof coat for warmth; see above.

Drop Ear – An ear in which the tip of the ear folds over and hangs down; not prick or erect

Entropion – A genetic disorder resulting in the upper or lower eyelid turning in

Fancier – A person who is especially interested in a particular breed or dog sport

Fawn – A red-yellow hue of brown

Feathering – A long fringe of hair on the ears, tail, legs, or body of a dog

Groom – To brush, trim, comb or otherwise make a dog's coat neat in appearance

Heel – To command a dog to stay close by its owner's side

Hip Dysplasia – A condition characterized by the abnormal formation of the hip joint

Inbreeding – The breeding of two closely related dogs of one breed

Glossary of Terms

Kennel – A building or enclosure where dogs are kept

Litter – A group of puppies born at one time

Markings – A contrasting color or pattern on a dog's coat

Mask – Dark shading on the dog's foreface

Mate – To breed a dog and a bitch

Neuter – To castrate a male dog or spay a female dog

Pads – The tough, shock-absorbent skin on the bottom of a dog's foot

Parti-Color – A coloration of a dog's coat consisting of two or more definite, well-broken colors; one of the colors must be white

Pedigree – The written record of a dog's genealogy going back three generations or more

Pied – A coloration on a dog consisting of patches of white and another color

Prick Ear – Ear that is carried erect, usually pointed at the tip of the ear

Puppy – A dog under 12 months of age

Purebred – A dog whose sire and dam belong to the same breed and who are of unmixed descent

Saddle – Colored markings in the shape of a saddle over the back; colors may vary

Shedding – The natural process whereby old hair falls off the dog's body as it is replaced by new hair growth.

Glossary of Terms

Sire – The male parent of a dog

Smooth Coat – Short hair that is close-lying

Spay – The surgery to remove a female dog's ovaries, rendering her incapable of breeding

Trim – To groom a dog's coat by plucking or clipping

Undercoat – The soft, short coat typically concealed by a longer outer coat

Vaccine – a shot that is given to a dog to help produce immunity to a specific disease.

Wean – The process through which puppies transition from subsisting on their mother's milk to eating solid food

Whelping – The act of birthing a litter of puppies

Glossary of Terms

Index

A

acquire 14
age 183
aggression 119
appearance 197
attributes 8
award 196

B

barking 110
bathing 78
bedding 47
behavior 17
birth 186
bitch 199
body 5, 199
breed 3
breeder 14
breeding 182

C

cage 198
canine 4
castrate 199
characteristics 10
chewing 120

Index

children 61
choking 171
clicker 102
coat 75, 199
collar 48, 98
coloration 199
colors 9, 199
comb 198
come 81
command 198
commands 81
communication 142
condition 198
crate 53

D

dam 198, 199
development 190
digging 121
disorder 198
double coat 197
down 82

E

ears 10, 77
eating 200
equipment 43
exercise 6
eyes 9

Index

F

face	197
feeding	67
female	182, 196, 200
first aid	51
food	46
foot	199

G

games	143
gene	197
genealogy	199
genetic	198
grooming	49, 74
growth	199

H

habitat	40
hair	199
handling	34
harness	97
health	67
healthy	37, 168
heel	85
heredity	11
hip	198
history	2
home	60
house	197, 198
housedog	6

Index

Photo Credits

Page 2, marialba.italia via Canva.com (Canva Pro License)

https://www.canva.com/photos/MAEEvA75k4k-greyhound/

Page 13, animalinfo via Canva.com (Canva Pro License)

https://www.canva.com/photos/MADstEAmgIg-italian-greyhound-puppies/

Page 40, AkikoCampbell via Canva.com (Canva Pro License)

https://www.canva.com/photos/MAEL2rOmTgA/

Page 67, violet-blue via Canva.com (Canva Pro License)

https://www.canva.com/photos/MADx40hRE3I-italian-greyhound-dog-eating-food/

Page 74, eduardolopezcoronadophoto via Canva.com (Canva Pro License)

Photo Credits

https://www.canva.com/photos/MAD-AUBov8A-groomer-grooming-italian-greyhound-dog/

Page 79, mikedabell via Canva.com (Canva Pro License)

https://www.canva.com/photos/MAEEkOZ7Juk-training-a-lurcher/

Page 146, GaiBru_Photo via Canva.com (Canva Pro License)

https://www.canva.com/photos/MADm_mogU-s-veterinarian-doing-an-ophthalmologic-scan-of-a-greyhound/

Page 176, monicadoallo via Canva.com (Canva Pro License)

https://www.canva.com/photos/MADCirhdHm0-three-greyhound/

Page 181, claudiodoenitzperez via Canva.com (Canva Pro License)

https://www.canva.com/photos/MAC_QuhReds-italian-greyhound-puppie/

References

American Kennel Club n.d, accessed 8 January 2022, https://www.akc.org/dog-breeds/greyhound/

AZ Animals Staff 2022, accessed 8 January 2022, https://a-z-animals.com/animals/greyhound/

Breeding Business 2017, accessed 8 January 2022, https://breedingbusiness.com/breeding-greyhound-dogs/

Canna-Pet 2018, accessed 8 January 2022, https://canna-pet.com/articles/greyhound-training-tips/

Dog Breed Info n.d, accessed 5 January 2022, https://www.dogbreedinfo.com/greyhound.htm

Dog Friendly Scene n.d, accessed 5 January 2022, https://dogfriendlyscene.co.uk/history-of-the-greyhound-breed/

Dogtime.com n.d, accessed 5 January 2022, https://dogtime.com/dog-breeds/greyhound#/slide/1

Emily W. n.d, ASPCA, accessed 8 January 2022, https://www.aspcapetinsurance.com/resources/greyhounds/

Emma Bowdrey n.d, Four Long Legs, accessed 5 January 2022, https://fourlonglegs.com/greyhounds/top-tips-for-training-your-retired-greyhound/

References

Greyhound Racing Victoria n.d, accessed 8 January 2022, https://greyhoundcare.grv.org.au/breeding/successful-breeding/

Greyhound Training n.d, accessed 8 January 2022, http://www.greyhoundtraining.net/greyhound-obedience.html

Greyhound Trust n.d, ASPCA, accessed 8 January 2022, https://www.greyhoundtrust.org.uk/home-a-greyhound/all-about-greyhounds

Hillspet.com n.d, accessed 5 January 2022, https://www.hillspet.com/dog-care/dog-breeds/greyhound

Hk9 Staff 2014, Highland Canine, accessed 8 January 2022, https://highlandcanine.com/about-the-breed-greyhound/

Indian Trail Animal Hospital n.d, accessed 5 January 2022, https://www.indiantrailanimalhospital.com/services/dogs/breeds/greyhound

Jay 2020, Breeding Business, accessed 5 January 2022, https://breedingbusiness.com/greyhound-racing-training/

Jenna Stregowski 2021, The Spruce Pets, accessed 8 January 2022, https://www.thesprucepets.com/breed-profile-greyhound-1117972

Linley Sanders 2022, Daily Paws, accessed 8 January 2022, https://www.dailypaws.com/dogs-puppies/dog-breeds/greyhound

References

MetLife Pet Insurance 2016, MetLife, accessed 8 January 2022, https://www.petfirst.com/breed-spotlights/greyhound/

Michele Welton 2021, YourPureBredPuppy.com, accessed 8 January 2022, https://www.yourpurebredpuppy.com/reviews/greyhounds.html

Michelle Schenker 2022, Love Your Dog, accessed 8 January 2022, https://www.loveyourdog.com/greyhound/

National Greyhound Association n.d, accessed 5 January 2022, https://www.ngagreyhounds.com/Greyhounds-As-Pets

Petfinder n.d, accessed 5 January 2022, https://www.petfinder.com/dog-breeds/greyhound/

PetMD n.d, accessed 5 January 2022, https://www.petmd.com/dog/breeds/c_dg_greyhound

Petplan n.d, accessed 5 January 2022, https://www.petplan.co.uk/pet-information/dog/breed/greyhound/

Purina n.d, accessed 5 January 2022, https://www.purina.co.uk/find-a-pet/dog-breeds/greyhound

The Kennel Club n.d, accessed 5 January 2022, https://www.thekennelclub.org.uk/search/breeds-a-to-z/breeds/hound/greyhound/

References

Vetsreet n.d, accessed 5 January 2022, http://www.vetstreet.com/dogs/greyhound

Wag Labs Inc. n.d, accessed 5 January 2022, https://wagwalking.com/breed/greyhound

www.ingramcontent.com/pod-product-compliance
Lightning Source LLC
Chambersburg PA
CBHW071311110426
42743CB00042B/1278